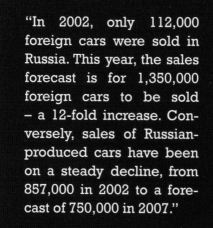

"In 2002, only 112,000 foreign cars were sold in Russia. This year, the sales forecast is for 1,350,000 foreign cars to be sold – a 12-fold increase. Conversely, sales of Russian-produced cars have been on a steady decline, from 857,000 in 2002 to a forecast of 750,000 in 2007."

— Jochen Legewie

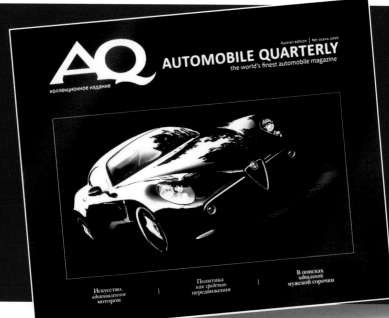

There will be many similarities and differences in the *AQ* you now hold and the Russian-produced version. For example: The finished Russian book is a "soft cover" instead of our familiar cloth over binder's board; substantial advertising pages lace editorial content; and newsstand sales are expected to be a major source of distribution.

SHARING THE TREASURE

Few countries or cultures can boast of an automotive history and heritage as rich as that enjoyed by the United States. The pioneering genius of a legion of players, ranging from early pioneers such as Henry Ford to the contemporary likes of Bob Lutz, has produced a tapestry of leaders in invention, innovation, manufacturing and marketing that constitutes the fabric of this dynamic industry and remains the envy and inspiration of the modern world.

In the spirit of "sharing our treasure" of automotive historical information, I am pleased to announce the news of our latest international expansion of the words

and images of *AQ/Automobile Quarterly* into the heartland of Russia. Our new international publishing partner is Mediacrat Publishing, which prides itself as being "artists of the magazine business." Our content is delivered via electronic files and then translated and blended into a splendid editorial product for the new emerging Russian market class possessing both wealth and a substantial intellectual curiosity.

This influential core group has a ravenous appetite for the legend and lore of the automobile such as what *AQ* has produced since its inception and founding by Scott Bailey in 1962. Mediacrat publisher Arman

Jilavian reports having already received many positive comments from advertisers and readers alike. We both agree that the best is yet to come.

Drive in Peace

Gerry Durnell

Gerry Durnell, Editor & Publisher

Automobile Quarterly

The Connoisseur's Publication of Motoring
– *Today, Yesterday, and Tomorrow* –

GERRY DURNELL
Editor & Publisher

KAYE BOWLES-DURNELL
Associate Publisher

JOHN C. DURNELL
Chief Operations Officer, Technical Editor

TRACY POWELL
Managing Editor

JOHN EVANS
Chief Financial Officer

DAN BULLEIT
Art Director

ROD HOTTLE
Administrative Assistant

ROBIN JEFFERS
Customer Service

L. SCOTT BAILEY
Founding Editor and Publisher

Contributing Photographers
MICHAEL FURMAN
FERDINAND HEDIGER
DAN LYONS
MICHEL ZUMBRUNN

Contributing Writers
BROOKS BRIERLEY
LEIGH DORRINGTON
FERDINAND HEDIGER
MAURICE HENDRY
KARL LUDVIGSEN

www.autoquarterly.com

ISBN 1-59613-054-7
(978-1-59613-054-8)

Printed in Korea

Contents

VOLUME 47, NUMBER 2 • SECOND QUARTER 2007

Cover: "58 Chevy"

Left: "Miss Bentley"

The J. Hebert Newport Phenomenon

O ne of the lesser-known contributors to Classic Era automotive design is Jesse Herbert Newport, Jr. (1906-1978). Often referred to as J. Herbert Newport or Herb Newport, his design career began at the Brunn & Co. coachbuilding firm in Buffalo, N.Y., at the age of 20. By the time his life ended, Newport had both given up and reclaimed an automotive career, changing from automobiles to freelance industrial design, then returning to automobiles. We know him best for his work at Duesenberg from 1933 to 1935, but he did much more.

BY BROOKS T. BRIERLEY

A Chicago native, Newport grew up wanting to draw cars. His father encouraged him, buying some drawing tools, which he used his entire life. By the early 1920s Newport had completed three years of college and still wanted to be a designer. But college did not teach automobile design. So he went along Chicago's automobile row on Michigan Avenue and asked dealers for a body builder chassis layout. Most were unwilling to give him one. The Lanchester dealer made one available and that led to his first sketch. Eventually half a dozen drawings of different makes, such as a Packard phaeton, were made. One was sent to Buffalo coachbuilder Brunn & Co. He was hired soon thereafter.

Newport was at Brunn for 10 months, designing two fenders and some other car parts. The first thing he designed was the Stearns-Knight eight-cylinder front fender and the pan on the rear end.

The beginnings of Newport's style are revealed in a convertible berline (a model sometimes described as a transformable) body on a 1930 Lincoln L chassis built by Philadelphia coachbuilder Alexander Wolfington, Son and Co. for D. B. Wentz Jr. of Rydal, Penn. The thick beltline is especially telling. So is the fabric top treatment. "I wanted a convertible top to look like a phaeton," Newport later recalled. That meant having the edge of the top extend beyond the body, not too tailored.

After his stint at Brunn, Newport went to work for the Floyd-Derham Co. on Jan. 1, 1929. The previous year, the death of Joseph Derham, founder of the Philadelphia coachbuilding business Derham Body Company, led to differences among his sons about the direction of the business. One son, Philip, who Newport described as an excellent body engineer and custom-body salesman, joined with an imported-car dealer, William Floyd, to create Floyd-Derham Co. (The work of Floyd-Derham was displayed in Floyd's Bryn Mawr showroom.) A number of Derham employees joined the new firm, including designer Bob Moses. It was not long before Moses went on to General Motors. Newport knew Moses from Chicago; that led to an introduction to Philip Derham. Soon,

Above: This view of Jack Dempsey's two-tone green transformable, on a 1929 duPont Model G chassis, emphasizes body details such as the beautiful rear fender shape and elegant door handles. The telltale transformable seam is clearly visible in the roof. Right: In January 1933, Newport completed this steering wheel design incorporating all the essential gauges and instruments of a dashboard (then called an instrument board).

Newport took Moses' place.

Floyd-Derham had a tenuous existence. The beginnings of the Depression took place in March 1929, when there was a severe stock market correction that effectively limited the series-custom orders that were so important to the new firm. Derham's plan was to have bodies built in England to make them appear more exclusive, but that did not work. At the same time, Floyd's retail car business had serious problems. These factors soon ended Floyd-Derham, after building about 15 to 20 bodies.

At Floyd-Derham, Newport once recalled, "We did a lot of nice jobs." Newport's first "nice job" was a Stutz Blackhawk in two shades of blue. Soon, he drew a limousine for a Lincoln L chassis and a station wagon

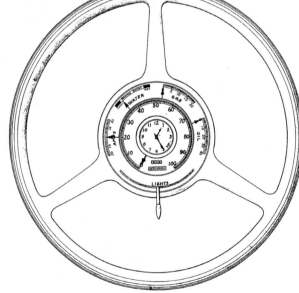

INSTRUMENTS IN STEERING WHEEL ELIMINATING INSTRUMENT BOARD

made to look like an old-fashioned coach. It had metal side panels, painted black with orange striping, set on an older Isotta-Fraschini chassis. It was "a real station wagon," Newport emphasized, meant for picking up guests at the railroad station to take to the estate. "The seats in the rear ran fore and aft," he added, and were entered from a rear door.

Another of his Floyd-Derham cars was a series-custom transformable, an open car whose top could be used in both convertible sedan or town car configurations, on a duPont chassis for movie star Charles "Buddy" Rogers. He ordered the car in dark blue with dark blue wire wheels and a blue leather interior, tweaked with a ball gearshift knob finished to look like a big pearl. A similar car, finished in two shades of green, was built for prize-fighter Jack Dempsey, who forgot about the need for a cushion fitting to ensure seat proportions were correct for his shape. He was not comfortable in the rear seat. The car was resold.

The duPont build records survive, revealing some

Floyd-Derham construction details. The transformable vee-shaped windshields were made by Rostand, who also made castings for coachbuilder Rollston. Five transformables are believed to have been built, the first two with a flat radiator shell. The last three, finished after Floyd-Derham closed, were completed by Merrimac, with duPont's rounded speedster-style front. In these last cars, likely sold as 1930 models, Newport tweaked the design into the "Royal town car," adding a swept panel that could allow two-toning.

Sometimes, the client could act as designer. The unusual sweep panel on a Duesenberg phaeton was drawn by the car's owner, John Eberson, a movie theater designer. "That's the way he wanted it," stated Newport, explaining to enthusiasts how it happened. He also pointed out that Eberson set seat specifications, too: the cushions were very soft, layered with three inches of down inside leather, a three-inch cushion of air and a three inch cushion of springs, a combination Newport once admitted was a bit too soft to

be a practical driver's seat.

When Floyd-Derham folded in September 1929, duPont asked Newport to help the transition and join them. It was a very short relationship – from September to November – during which time he also did some catalog work, such as sketches for the 1930 automobile shows. Then the effects of the October 1929 stock market crash began to be felt.

By February 1930, Newport was in Detroit, working at Dietrich, Inc., which was part of the mass bodybuilder Murray Corporation. With shrinking series-custom coachbuilding orders, Dietrich became a design studio for Murray customers, such as Ford. Newport was there until October 1930, enough time to accomplish, as he later put it, "one good deed": the rear quarter window of the 1931 Ford Victoria, pivoted to clear the rear wheel housing. After being laid off, Newport found work at General Motors, doing small parts designs, such as ash trays and lights. Cutbacks came to GM the following year and Newport was

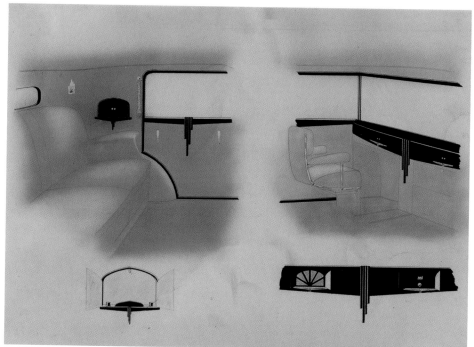

Shown here, Newport's 1934 town car proposal for Mae West revised an earlier Walter Murphy body design. The split windshield and rear window stand out, as does the extra taillight. More elaborate proposals were made to Miss West but were also rejected.

again looking for work.

That took him to Studebaker in the summer of 1931. He began there continuing to draw car parts. Later, he drew a streamlined body on a Commander chassis. There was some company interest in this and he went on to make a one-eighth clay model of it. Studebaker controlled Pierce-Arrow then and was doing a lot of their design work. The rear-end design was adapted for the back of the famous 1933 Silver Arrow show car. Enthusiasts will recall the Silver Arrow was originally drawn by Phil Wright, set on Pierce's long 147-inch wheelbase chassis. Studebaker wanted the car on the shorter 139-inch wheelbase chassis it made for Pierce.

The most pleasing way to shorten the body was to break the rear deck with a truncated window, as in Newport's model. Wright is said never to have forgiven that change in his design but his furor was aimed not at Newport but at Studebaker's head designer, James R. Hughes.

At the end of 1932, Studebaker made a Draconian reduction in the design section. Newport went back to Chicago, where he continued to make design proposals. One was a steering wheel that combined all dashboard instruments – eliminating the dash board. Then came a call from Duesenberg. Gordon Buehrig had just left and they needed a stylist. The reference

came from a familiar name: Philip Derham had joined Duesenberg in the spring of 1930 and was in charge of their custom body department.

DUESENBERG

There must have been considerable soul searching at the Auburn Automobile Company after Fred Duesenberg's untimely death in 1932. The supply of Model J chassis was running out and needed to be replaced, yet the Depression clearly signaled that updating the Model J supercar would not be

This 1933 Duesenberg Model J is one of five Derham convertible sedans built for Duesenberg. It was originally one of two SJ models built and was illustrated in the 1934 Indy 500 race program as SJ-507. The original owner was H.G. Leibhardt, the man behind the financing for the Floyd-Derham 1934-35 Ford fabric-bodied sport coupes, with which Newport was intimately involved.

economic. In the works was a plan to reposition the marque more towards Lincoln and Cadillac, with a factory-bodied streamlined model.

Newport joined Duesenberg in February 1933. Alex Tremulis (later of Tucker fame) was hired as his assistant. They quickly brought streamlining to Duesenberg. The makeover included a new radiator shell. However, Newport's first design job there was modest: the interior of E.L. Cord's Willoughby-bodied Model J limousine.

Duesenberg was never a large company. Some visitors to the factory remarked at how compact such a famous business was. In the mid-1930s it was very lean, indeed. That required lots of multitasking among employees, including Newport. Among his assignments was taking official photographs of the cars, what we now call "factory photographs." When the Brunn Riviera convertible sedan, Duesenberg's display

Above: The stunning Walker-LaGrande coupe, Duesenberg J-554, was built for Indianapolis pharmecutical owner Eli Lilly in 1934 on Duesenberg's short 142-inch wheelbase chassis. The car survives and still looks like new. Right: A close look at the radiator shell details of the Walker-LaGrande coupe. Top: Another J, this one J-534 of 1934 vintage, is a rear view of this story's lead photo.

for the 1934 automobile shows, was not finished in time for the factory photographic process, Newport made a drawing of the car to accompany the media publicity releases.

Some of Newport's work at Duesenberg included enhancing existing designs. His proposed town car for Mae West, then the highest-paid motion picture star in Hollywood, adapted a leftover Walter Murphy series-custom town car body that Franklin Hershey designed at the end of the 1920s. In limiting the proposal to details such as changing the hanging of the rear door from front to rear, a new rear apron, and new windshield and window treatments, Newport may have underestimated West, who was also a savvy businesswoman and very much a car enthusiast. He never met her during this process, something that may also have worked against him. So it was no surprise when

This 1935 Duesenberg JN was bodied by Rollston and later modified by Bohman & Schwartz for Clark Gable. Gable ordered this special convertible coupe after seeing Newport's design on a similar coupe made for Gary Cooper.

The second version of the Aeronaut was built on a 1935 Ford V8 chassis. Details of the Aeronaut's interior (right) are intriguing – such as the patterned metal door sill mimicking a "Duesenberg Special" feature.

West later rejected Newport's completely custom-built Duesenberg town car design using his own flamboyant, bulbous style. Fortunately, this second design proposal for West became the basis for the town car built for candy heiress, Ethel Mars.

A one-of-a-kind streamlined two-passenger coupe built in 1934 on Duesenberg's J-554 short 145-inch wheelbase chassis for Eli Lilly Jr. of Indianapolis may be the apogee of Herb Newport's Classic Era style. Like many custom designs of the time, it includes characteristics borrowed from other marques, such as 1934 Cadillac/LaSalle bumpers. Pierce-Arrow's fender-mounted headlight patent expired at this time, encouraging Newport to create a version located, not at the crown as Pierce did, but lower, at the most forward point of the fender. The headlights were intended to be flush with the fender but there was not enough time to have glass specially cast. So they were set in a thick bezel to stick out of the fender.

The pontoon racing-style fenders were one of

Newport's design themes. Newport later recalled that Lilly liked the car very much but did not keep it very long. A crowd would always gather around the coupe when parked, making it difficult to get to – something Lilly did not like.

The coupe's streamlined body included a new radiator shell, one that would be seen on other Duesenbergs of the time. The radiator grille had the slight vee-shape of earlier Duesenberg Js, stretching forward over the front axle. That required each brass strip in the grille – measuring 1/8 x 3/4-inch thick and each a different length – to be individually bent with spacers between each rod. Newport reported they were handmade at a cost of $500 with another $500 paid for plating (copper, nickel and chrome) – an impressive sum when a new Ford listed for $500. The total body cost was about $21,000. Coachbuilder A. H. Walker built the body in the Weymann factory in Indianapolis, which was credited to Duesenberg's in-house label LaGrande.

Newport considered his "masterpiece" the "Mormon

Meteor," a gigantic race car built on the 142 1/2-inch SJ wheelbase chassis at the Duesenberg factory for David "Ab" Jenkins in 1934-35. First named "the Duesenberg Special," it was designed for the Utah Salt Flats (now called Bonneville) for record-breaking runs in August 1935. Everything about the car was speedy, including its style and the process to make it.

Ab Jenkins came into the factory one Saturday morning. He went upstairs and met with Duesenberg president Harold Ames about building a car that could be both street legal as well as ready for racing. Jenkins returned to Indianapolis the following Saturday morning. In the interim, Newport created the car's exterior design on paper. Newport later remembered Jenkins making a minor adjustment in the rear fender step plate location but otherwise approving everything.

Duesenberg still had the internal capability to shape metal – the shop foreman, Sam Regan, was considered a master worker of aluminum – so the racing body was made there. Not only could Newport see the car taking shape, he had the ability to guide the metal-shaping process and make any corrections right on the spot. As the car neared completion, Augie Duesenberg called to Newport to come down from his second floor work

became an enormous limousine-landaulet weighing almost four tons. It began as a limousine proposal for the Shah of Persia. The Shah's son spent several weeks at the Duesenberg factory while the limousine design

his design as "ruined."

Another project was the Model Q. Duesenberg planned to go to a more modern format than the J; what became the Cord 810 was originally intended to

Above: This interesting town-car sketch for a Packard chassis included headlights set in flush in the front fenders (as he intended for the 1934 Duesenberg Walker coupe) and bulbous fender wells seen in the West/Mars Duesenberg town car. Right: Newport in a formal portrait later in his life.

area to see the motor. Augie started it up, revving the engine to 5000 rpm to produce 400 hp. It did not have a muffler. Newport once recalled that the noise from the engine "shook the entire building."

By July 1935 the car was at the salt flats being tuned for a run. The following month the Duesenberg Special recorded speeds as high as 153.97 mph.

Another famous Newport Duesenberg was a very different concept, this one a short-wheelbase (125-inch) supercharged roadster, having a blue-gray body. It was built in 1936 for motion picture star Gary Cooper. Cooper owned a 1930 Duesenberg sport phaeton but liked to race and wanted a faster car. Clark Gable, Cooper's friend, liked racing, too, and had a similar speedster built for him. While uncharacteristic of Newport's streamlined work of the time, the speedsters have great style, and signaled Duesenberg's return to more classic body shapes for its last line of cars.

The largest of Newport's Duesenberg designs

was being developed. It was never ordered. The drawings led to John Wuest Hunt, a West Coast follower of Father Divine, to order it for the leader of his cult. The car was set on a stretched 178-inch wheelbase chassis, so wide – some of the body extends beyond the running boards – as to offer four-abreast seating. Its $28,000 cost and "throne car" designation allowed it to become notorious even before completion.

During construction at Bohman & Schwartz's Pasadena shops in the spring of 1937, Hunt was wanted for violations of the Mann Act, a law that prohibited so-called white slavery and banned the interstate transport of females for "immoral purposes." Federal marshals guarded the car, hoping to capture Hunt if he tried to inspect it. Hunt successfully registered the car in his religious name, "John the Baptist," with a Beverly Hills address. The throne car made the newspapers with its final mechanical check in October 1937. Newport did not like the end result, describing

do that. The Q, powered by a version of the Auburn V12 engine, continued the development direction. It was to have an automatic transmission. Newport did some sketches. It never went further than a one-eighth scale model.

THE AERONAUT

Concurrent with his Duesenberg work, Newport collaborated with Philip Derham for a sport coupe body for Ford's 112-inch wheelbase V8 chassis. Customizing Fords had been big business in the early 1920s when body builders such as Paco and Bub stirred imaginations with their rakish coupes and racing bodies. The Depression suggested reviv-

concept with a complete visual modification on Ford's 1935 chassis, which incidentally included a radiator shell suggestive of the Newport's Duesenbergs. But before that happened, the 1934 car's short life included a great anecdote of a trial run with Newport driving the car on Saturday afternoon to Lafayette, Ind., for a football game. A new LaSalle roadster came alongside and there was a short race. "We walked away from that LaSalle," he recalled. The Aeronaut "really went."

Philip Derham took one of the 1935 cars to Hollywood. An actress, accustomed to the features of her husband's 1933 Pierce-Arrow coupe, was said to be openly critical. Her reaction suggested the Aeronaut would not generate interest in the movie colony. Even so, production began with three – or 10, depending on the source of information – cars built. The next plan was to publicize them as the 1935 Indianapolis 500 pace car. Before that could happen, the project's backer had an accident in one of the cars. His help quickly ceased. The Aeronaut became history and none are believed to survive.

Newport's last prewar automotive work involved

The 1937 "Throne Car" was eventually owned by Father Divine, a controversial figure that called much attention to this car. The Duesenberg limousine was an expensive venture, the end result a "ruined" design, according to Newport.

ing this economical concept, although there was now added risk of adapting to the annual model styling changes. The Aeronaut body was built like an airplane with paneled wood over a wood frame and a linen finish skin, painted to look like metal. "A stationary Weymann" body Newport once called it, referring to the once-popular Weymann fabric bodies. That light construction with a V8 engine provided an impressive power-to-weight ratio. It was to be called Aeronaut, an accolade then given to pilots with special accomplishments. Aeronaut prototypes were built in the Weymann factory in Indianapolis, which also produced some Duesenberg bodies. Prices of $2,500 to $3,500 were expensive for the time – a supercharged Auburn V8 speedster listed for $2,245, a number of Pierce-Arrow models cost less than $3,000.

The first Aeronaut was built on a 1934 Ford chassis. It provided a streamlined coupe body using the standard Ford hood and front fenders. When the 1935 Fords came out the design was revised to change the

less-exotic assignments. He went to work for General Motors' Pontiac Division in February 1936. "I managed to accomplish something," he wrote in a resume for the Auburn-Cord-Duesenberg Club. "The 1938 Pontiac was about 95 percent my design."

In the summer of 1937 George Walker asked Newport to help with the Nash-Kelvinator account. That included both cars and appliances: a Leonard refrigerator, a Kelvinator washing machine, the 1939 Nash cars. They worked in the Kelvinator plant in Detroit, not at the Nash factory in Kenosha, Wis. Newport later recalled his experience at Nash with some frustration. The lines for the 1939 model were originally developed with the front fender running into the door. As the economics of the new design were reviewed, an order came down to use 1938 door panels as an economy, forcing a rework of an existing design. Newport was obviously disappointed, particularly when remembering how design issues were resolved at Duesenberg or when the cost of plating a single radiator grille equaled the cost of a new Ford or

Plymouth. Yet, this approach was how Nash survived the Depression.

After working at Nash Newport did some freelance work, as varied as custom-body designs and bumper accessories and turn signals, and in May 1939 he joined Chrysler. He did the 1940 Plymouth front grille. One of his sketches, a drawing of wraparound louvers and disappearing headlights, caught someone's eye as it found its way to becoming the front of the Chrysler Thunderbolt.

For his own use, Newport bought a Lincoln Zephyr, then left Chrysler in July 1940.

Of all his moving around, one of the consistencies in Newport's automotive career was working with Philip Derham. A detailed discussion of their relationship, written or on tape, has yet to be discovered. Fortunately, they continued to collaborate off and on into the early 1940s. A handsome drawing prophesizing what became the 1940 Plymouth front end was produced in June 11, 1939, under the title "Newport and Derham, Styling for Industry." Some of these

drawings, which appear as color drawings on a blackboard, included a smart-looking logo: an orange-red ribbon across the bottom of the drawing, lettered in black. Their partnership was last rekindled in July 1940. Derham had returned to Philadelphia's Main Line and the town of Rosemont, Penn., the home of the family Derham Company that he had left in the 1920s. There, Derham and Newport designed and built models of industrial items for Armstrong Cork Co.

A long resume that Newport recreated in his last years – which fortunately includes some curriculum vitae-like comments – points out that he liked to be with himself. That may explain his on-again off-again business relationship with Philip Derham, and the general shortness of his job assignments.

AFTER THE CLASSIC ERA

As World War II began, Newport tried to enlist in the military but said he was considered too old (he was in his mid 30s then). He moved to Wittman, Md., on the Eastern Shore, and established a model shop. The shop had capacity to fabricate plastic, something that continued to keep him very busy in the postwar period, too. He designed a vacuum-forming press for plastics, from which he made wing-tip lights for planes. Like other innovative designers of the time, he had a story about a machine design being taken by a large company and used without compensation.

Sometime after the war, a friend called and asked Newport if he would like to go to an Auburn-Cord-Duesenberg Club meet in Massachusetts. He said

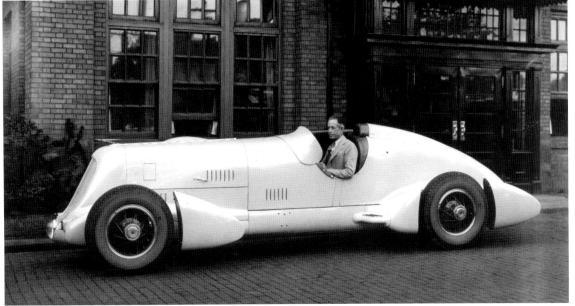

Ab Jenkins at the wheel of the "Duesenberg Special" in street-legal form in front of the Firestone Tire and Rubber Company headquarters in Akron, Ohio. The car in color, top right.

Above: Years later Newport stood in front of the "Mormon Meteor" displayed at a car show. Below: This drawing of a 1970 Lincoln Continental, modified as a Coupe de Ville, shows Newport understood modern automobile design; the trunk shape and taillight design reveal his Classic Era perspective.

yes. They drove up in a Duesenberg J. At the evening banquet, an announcement was made that someone important from the Duesenberg factory was in the room. Newport later recalled hearing that, adding he looked around the room to see who it was, not realizing he was the one about to be given the spotlight. The banquet led to his first speech.

That was also the beginning of a closer association with the car hobby. Sometime later, an enthusiast approached Newport, asking him to design a car body similar to the Gary Cooper short-wheelbase roadster. Newport happily drew it. The enthusiast soon returned, reporting that he could not find anyone to build the body. Newport realized he could build it in his own shop. That led to additional restorations and conversions, including reworking formal Classic Era body styles to informal open ones, mostly Duesenbergs

with an occasional other marque such as Cadillac or Rolls-Royce.

In addition, Newport did some parts finishing. He promoted engine-turned and damascene metal finishes. *Mechanix Illustrated* covered his work in a short story in 1965, which catapulted Newport into the restoration business. No one was restoring Cord instrument panels then; many were using plastic substitutes. Newport worked closely with a plater in Baltimore, finding there was a great deal of interest not only from those owning Auburn Automobile Co. cars but other classics as well. There were also individual finishing jobs such as the differential housing of a Bugatti and the valve cover of a Hispano-Suiza.

As Newport increasingly provided advice and information to a growing number of vintage car enthusiasts, he also participated in seminars and presentations at a number of car meets and museums. Recordings of these events reveal his audiences' fascination with everything Duesenberg. Questions often led Newport's discussion away from his days at Floyd-Derham and the Aeronaut car, as well as minimizing the discussions of Newport's own Duesenberg work, to focus on the best-known cars. Fortunately, all of Newport's Duesenbergs survive.

After a talk at a Classic Car Club function, attorney and author Louis Steinwedel approached Newport. He proposed doing a Duesenberg book through his publisher, Chilton. That led to co-authoring a very informative book titled "The Duesenberg". It was originally

The 1940-41 Chrysler Thunderbolts and Newport-Phaetons were Chrylser's effort at prewar showmanship. Alex Tremulis worked with Ralph Roberts to create a handful of concept cars, and Newport's influence is seen in the final disappearing-headlight treatment. Newport and Tremulis went back a few years, but Newport's stint at Chrysler was a short-lived affair.

published in 1970, with a Japanese-language version done later in the year. Newport decided to embellish the effort and had some of the books bound in leather, done locally in the nearby town of Easton. A larger, revised edition of the English version was published by W.W. Norton in 1982. This book's understated appearance and size make it easy to overlook, much like its author. Even so, it offers invaluable perspective on Duesenberg's streamlined period of design.

Over the years, Newport accumulated a good-sized collection of automotive materials, including extraordinary historic Classic Era photographs, many drawings and some tapes of his presentations. Recently, they were acquired by the Transportation History Collection in the Special Collections Library of the University of Michigan. Now, they complement the library's landmark Pierce-Arrow Collection to provide an important focal point for Classic Era automotive research.

Newport's greatest tribute is likely something not quite so scholarly. It is having all the Duesenbergs he designed survive, each running and looking like new.

AQ

POSEY
UNCONTROLLED
FORCE

A ny day with Sam Posey is an adventure. He is a fine artist, an architect, an author, an Emmy-winning broadcaster, and a successful racer. Perhaps no other driver of his era – even Dan Gurney – drove in more major racing series, went faster or can more ably relate firsthand the riotous days of the SCCA Can-Am series, Trans-Am and Formula 5000 than Sam Posey, let alone Le Mans, the FIA World Championship, the Indianapolis 500 and the USAC Champ Car circuit. He drove a Formula One car for world champion John Surtees, and once drove a NASCAR stock car for fabled owner Cotton Owens.

BY LEIGH DORRINGTON

As a racer he was sometimes brash, outspoken. He was one of the few drivers ever to leave Chris Economaki without a comeback. But as a spokesman for racing, no one is more articulate than Sam Posey.

Walking into the Connecticut studio he designed and shares with his wife, artist Ellen Greisedieck, the conversation begins like an avalanche. First, a glance around: bookshelves, everywhere; a drafting table; diecast cars; bottles of Newman's Own salad dressing; a book on WWI era battleships open on the table; floor plans, plot plans and colorful abstracts pinned to the wall. Where to begin? A casual question is asked, and everything rushes down at once.

It's all part of the same for Sam Posey.

The qualities of creative challenges – driving a race car, creating a painting or designing a house – follow the same process with Sam: a "blank canvas," uncontrolled forces brought to bear, and an ordered resolution. He is well qualified to speak on the subject; indeed, he spoke as a guest lecturer at the School of Architecture at Miami University in Oxford, Ohio, in 2006. But we are getting ahead of the story.

A CONNECTICUT YANKEE

Sam Posey grew up in a fun house. Although his mother, Mary, was widowed late in WWII and Sam never knew his father, recollections of his early days are of a household filled with fun and adventure in equal parts by his mother and grandmother. Not just a house but a large stone house on a hilltop in the northwest corner of Connecticut that today is home to the artist Jasper Johns. There was also an apartment in New York, where he attended school.

Vehicles were always part of his life. He recalls waking up at the age of 8 to the roar of a fire engine coming up the driveway to find that it was being driven by his mother, her brown hair flying. She had just bought the fire engine. A series of more or less interesting cars were always in the driveway. And there was Uncle Teddy's Wind Wagon. Refused permission by his parents to build an airplane in 1929, Mary's brother Teddy created the next best thing. He built an ungainly contraption out of angle iron with a Harley-Davidson motorcycle engine mounted high and in front of the driver. The three-wheeled device was pulled through the air by an airplane propeller.

Eventually his mother remarried, and Dr. Bill Moore came into Sam's life. Moore was a prominent New York vascular surgeon, often called out in the middle of the night and once called to the Middle East where he performed emergency surgery on the Shah of Iran.

In 1958 Sam and his mother traveled together to Europe. History, art and architecture were all a part of the trip, but Sam was totally engrossed with another

Left: Sam Posey's grandfather, a principal in a Hartford fire insurance company, constructed the stone house near Sharon, Conn. Right: Uncle Teddy's Wind Wagon remained in the family for decades and is now owned by the Lane Motor Museum in Nashville, Tenn.

Left: Erwin Henze (left) was Posey's first mechanic. He worked a garage in Sharon and had apprenticed with the Mercedes-Benz Grand Prix team before the war. Above: Posey in the Autodynamics D 9 Formula Vee at the Nassau Speed Week, December 1966.

discovery – motor racing. A copy of Mike Hawthorne's "Challenge Me the Race" was all the primer he needed. On his next trip to Europe Sam visited the top racing circuits, patiently recording a lap of each with a series of photographs taken exactly 100 feet apart.

By this time a sprawling, contemporary home had been constructed on the hilltop within site of the stone house for the growing Moore family. Sam and his friend Johnnie Whitman constructed an elaborate gravity track for racing small cars in the enormous basement of the new house, which he described in his autobiography "The Mudge Pond Express", audaciously published when Sam was only 32 years old. Gravity racing in the basement was replaced with a new challenge when Posey and Whitman began spending hours propelling themselves around the cement floor on a wheeled device steered from the front like a sled, called the Mudge Pond Express after the nearby pond and which gave its name to the book.

Bicycle races on a tough 6.15 mile course that circled Mudge Pond then became the competition of choice. At first a full lap would take over an hour, timed by one competitor sitting under a tree enjoying a sandwich while the other rode for all he was worth. Later an elaborate set of rules and procedures emerged.

The Moores' dinner guests were always interesting. But one in particular was of special interest to Sam, John Fitch, still the only American to drive for a Mercedes-Benz factory racing team (*Automobile Quarterly*, Vol. 44 No. 2). Fitch was a neighbor and sometimes dinner guest in Connecticut. Posey also described in his autobiography how he managed to be seated next to the accomplished racer, hoping that Fitch would recognize a fellow driver and future world champion in Posey.

Although he didn't know it then, this happy background would shape Posey's life.

THE RACING LIFE

Because Posey became a public figure first as a racer, we'll begin there as well. Not surprisingly, Posey's first racing experience came at Lime Rock Park. The track was built in 1957 in Lakeville, Conn., close to Posey's home.

The first outing at Lime Rock was a test in a Formcar Formula Vee imported by none other than John Fitch. His driving career progressed quickly, first in an Alfa-Romeo at Bridgehampton in 1965 with Harry Theodoracopulous and Bob Grossman and then with his own Porsche 904 at Daytona and Watkins Glen in 1966. A trip to the Bahamas with his Formula Vee race car for the end-of-the-year Speed Week in 1965 proved to be prescient when Posey met fellow racer Ray Caldwell, creator of the fledgling Autodynamics Formula Vee. The two got on well and in Caldwell Posey saw an eager, innovative mind with whom he could build his own program.

Risking his inheritance, Posey invested in the partnership. Initially, the plan was to design and build their own sports racing car but the introduction of the SCCA's Can-Am series changed that. Posey was on the Can-Am grid for the first race at St. Jovite in September 1966 in a McLaren-Ford.

By 1967 the pair decided that the way to go in the wide-open SCCA Can-Am series was to develop and build their own car for the 1968 season. That car – the Caldwell D 7 – was typical of the series. Motivated by the chance to establish himself as a top-rank designer and the challenge to put down the enormous power of the V-8 engines that defined the series, Caldwell built the car around solid axles. The aerodynamics of the car closely resembled the shape of the McLaren M6A that debuted the same year. But the results could not have been more different. While the McLaren relied on a proven, simple chassis design and extensive test program, the Caldwell relied on an unproven concept and suffered throughout its career from a lack of development.

During the same time, the SCCA's Trans-Am series for sedans became a hotbed of direct competition between Detroit manufacturers. Roger Penske's successful partnership with driver Mark Donohue and Chevrolet propelled them to the front ranks of American racing, winning the Trans-Am championship in 1968 and 1969. Posey was called on to drive Penske's second Camaro in 1968, essentially to protect a championship for Penske and Donohue. In 1969, he filled in for Peter Revson – who was racing at Indianapolis – and won the Memorial Day race at Lime Rock in a Shelby Mustang.

For the 1970 Trans-Am series Chrysler Corporation came calling, seeking a team to prepare and race the Dodge Challenger against Penske's dominant Chevrolet team, the Ford teams of Shelby and Bud Moore, and Dan Gurney's Plymouth Barracudas. Posey and Caldwell established a race shop on the West Coast. Their lime green Challenger with a black vinyl roof was a favorite of the crowd and Posey finished fourth in the championship.

Formula 5000 provided a stage on which Posey was highly successful. Still racing with Ray Caldwell, the team entered the 1969 SCCA Formula 5000 series with an Eagle and later a McLaren and the steadfast support of chief mechanic Jack McCormack throughout a difficult season, finishing second in the championship. In 1971 Posey and McCormack formed a new team with connecting rod-maker Fred Carrillo. Seeking to gain an advantage in the series the team selected the Surtees TS#8 chassis, built by world champion John Surtees.

Posey was locked in a battle for the championship with David Hobbs throughout the 1971 season, with Hobbs taking the championship in the final race. Posey finished second again for the 1972 championship in a Surtees TS 11 to New Zealander Graham McRae. Posey drove for Dan Gurney to develop the 1974 Eagle F5000 car, but an unexpected opportunity found him as a car constructor in partnership with McCormack and McRae for the 1974 season building and racing a car they called the Talon. The car was fast, but finished only one race due to a series of engine problems.

Working with Surtees rekindled Posey's boyhood dream of becoming a world champion. Surtees nominated Posey as a reserve driver for the U.S. Grand Prix at Watkins Glen in 1971. Posey won the start by beating Le Mans winner Gijs van Lennep by more than three seconds in a test. Although Posey was inexperienced in Formula One, he learned that he could race with the best drivers in the world. He drove for Team

Left: Posey met artist Alexander Calder as an art student and later competed in the Calder BMW Art Car at Le Mans in 1975. Right: Posey in the Surtees TS 8 Formula 5000 car at Laguna Seca in 1971.

Surtees at Watkins Glen again in 1972.

Posey also competed for Luigi Chinetti's Ferrari North American Racing Team in the major endurance races at Le Mans, Sebring and Daytona, as well as other American races. While today Posey describes the drives as "a busman's holiday," he finished third at Le Mans in a Ferrari 512M in 1971 with Tony Adamowicz after setting fastest lap of the race – in the real-life Porsche-Ferrari battle made famous by Steve McQueen's movie "Le Mans".

The Indianapolis 500 was Posey's next challenge. The 1972 race saw the introduction of a radically new Indy Eagle, one of the first of a new breed of Indy cars to capitalize on the advantages of new aerodynamic developments. Posey qualified seventh in an Eagle as the fastest rookie in the race, while veteran Bobby Unser stunned the Indy establishment in another Eagle by raising the qualifying record by 17 mph over the pre-

Top: Posey was the fastest-qualifying and highest-finishing rookie in the 1972 Indianapolis 500, won by Mark Donohue. Above: At the 12 Hours of Sebring in 1971, Posey drove a NART Ferrari 512S with Ronnie Bucknum. The pair was fourth after six hours when a tire blew, causing damage that took them out of the race. Right: Posey was second in the Formula 5000 Championship again in 1972, won by Graham McRae.

Paul Newman and Posey were teammates at Bob Sharp Racing in 1980. "The twin-turbo 300ZX was designed by Trevor Harris, but the car came out one year too late. The competition had already caught up."

vious year's record – the biggest jump in Speedway history. Posey finished fifth in the race, again the highest rookie, but curiously did not win the Rookie of the Year Award that typically goes to the top-finishing first-year driver. The race remains one of his greatest accomplishments and one of his biggest disappointments.

The ensuing years saw Posey become the only American driver on BMW's highly successful first foray into international competition. Posey won the 12 Hours of Sebring in 1975 driving with Hans Stuck and Ronnie Peterson and raced the BMW Art Car painted by Alexander Calder at Le Mans.

By 1975 Posey had driven in virtually every top racing series in the world. He was all of 31 years old.

AS ARTIST

But even before he was a racer Posey was an artist. Sitting in his studio, he describes how art is the one thing that has always identified him. "The thing that gave me my character at school was art. I was the kid who was always in the art room." And he was talented.

He studied at the prestigious Rhode Island School of Design in Providence. He was studying there when he began racing. He would sometimes work all night to complete art projects so that he could race on the weekend. With the racing partnership with Ray Caldwell flourishing, his priorities changed. He would return to the solitary challenges in his studio after the intensity of a race weekend.

Landscapes were what he painted until he suddenly faced a new challenge. In 1994 Posey was diagnosed with Parkinson's disease. "I didn't think I would be able to paint any more. I thought I would have to do something I would have to hover over." Instead he "started with collages, and I found myself very comfortable with pure abstraction.

"I discovered that abstract art had all the elements of traditional landscape painting." He gets up from his chair and returns with two art books to explain. The paintings of Edward Hopper are used to illustrate the

Left: The 1972 United States Grand Prix at Watkins Glen was Posey's second start for Team Surtees. He finished one second behind Graham Hill, a three-time winner of the USGP. Right: "The Challenger enabled me to be a part of the 1970 Trans-Am Series, which many people still consider the best year ever for an American road racing series."

traditional elements. "Paintings have a foreground, a mid-ground and a background. Figures and ground are relative to one another. There is a horizon line."

Then, a book of Wassily Kandinsky's work is brought out to illustrate abstraction. "Kandinsky began as a traditional landscape painter," Posey explained. Turning pages to show the evolution of Kandinsky's early work to his later abstract paintings, he becomes animated. "Suddenly you've synergized the entire picture plane. Gone is the element of perspective. There is no horizon line. No sense of one thing being in front of another. The paintings have a contemporary, 'all over' quality. Once you've seen this," pointing at Kandinsky, "you can't go back to that," with a nod toward Hopper. The Hopper book is taken off the table.

"I love Kandinsky. Look at how cool that is – that little form – how it is constantly changing its relationships with the other elements. When I was in Munich racing for BMW, the Stadtische Galerie had the world's greatest collection of Kandinsky. I'm afraid I often for-

got about racing and was fascinated with Kandinsky. I was making drawings all over the place."

His own later move to abstract painting was very productive. Although he only attempted two paintings of racing cars, they are startlingly original. "I was trying to paint the 'feeling' that the front of the car had as it turned into a corner." It is a unique perspective, one that comes from deep inside the driver's psyche.

Silkscreen prints of other Posey abstracts have been produced by master print-maker Ken Tyler, who printed works of artists Roy Lichstenstein, Frank Stella and Robert Motherwell. Posey's abstract paintings hang in the Tate in London, the Walker Art Center in Minneapolis and the National Museum of Australia in Canberra.

Happily, he has been able to continue to work on large canvasses. His "Battleships" paintings are an important new direction. "With the 'Battleships' I saw the opportunity to go back to straight painting. It's exciting to be involved in new projects. There is a moment when it's just a concept. Then it comes together.

"It's a lot like racing. When you go out on the track to begin with, the racing line, braking points, shift points have not been defined. The first few laps are getting up to g-forces. After about 10 laps it begins to hum. Then you're humming a little louder. And then it all comes together."

He points to one of the "Battleships" paintings. "This could be a lap – the line, the point where the car unwinds out of the turn, the centrifugal forces ... the woods rushing up ... the forces working against the car. That's what I'm looking for. Translating forces into something visual."

ARCHITECT

As with art – and racing for that matter – designing a house is highly visual. Perhaps it is no surprise, then, that Posey designed his first house for himself. "I had been living in California since

1970. We first set up a shop there for the Trans-Am program, and then Formula 5000 and the Indy team." By late 1973 he was working with Dan Gurney to develop the next generation Eagle Formula 5000 car.

"I'd been renting an apartment and property values were just skyrocketing at that time. When the rent went up again I realized that I could have a mortgage for the same amount every month." He bought a piece of property in San Juan Capistrano with his winnings from the 1972 Indianapolis 500, and took a mortgage to build a house. That first house strongly reflected the influence of architect Frank Lloyd Wright. It was very horizontal, with exaggerated overhangs and fit into its setting along the top of a cliff overlooking the ocean.

Posey began designing houses for others. He and Ellen returned to Connecticut in 1982 when their son, John, was born. He created a company called Posey Design, invested in designing and building spec houses and established a local reputation. That reputation became much wider when he was asked to design the infield buildings at Lime Rock Park. The first, the infield pavilion, is a simple clapboard structure built on the hillside with a large outdoor viewing terrace. Others followed in a similar style, but the building he designed with his brother David for the start-finish line has perhaps become his signature design.

Today he has designed some 80 houses and buildings. Many are in his corner of Connecticut, but others have been built in Massachusetts, Florida, Hawaii and Seattle. Although the style of Posey's architecture is typically vernacular, Wright's influence continues in his approach to design. The idea of "a box of air," uncontrolled forces and an ordered resolution is placed on the table. Wright frequently used the principles of "press and release": A person entering a Wright space might first pass through a very low or narrow space that suddenly opens up into a grander space the architect is leading them into.

Posey demonstrates with another book. Exploded drawings show a unique flow designed by Wright into each house. Sam's houses are similar, with an organic quality that grows from the entrance, beckoning back to the approach to the first lap, the blank canvas.

Top: In the ex-Siffert Vasek Pollak Porsche 917 PA at Riverside. "I was teamed with Milt Minter, and beating him. Vasek asked me to let Milt go ahead and paid me Milt's prize money." Bottom: John Whitman and Jack McCormack were stalwarts of Posey's racing career, seen here at a USAC Formula 5000 race at Seattle in 1971.

He has a special affinity for designing libraries. A recently completed project is a new library for the lower school at the nearby Indian Mountain School in Lakeville, Conn. Like all of his designs, the library fits comfortably into its space and is built with simple materials.

Posey also designed the home he and Ellen live in with John and daughter Judy. The house is just a bit further along the Connecticut hilltop from the contemporary house and the stone house that have been constants in his life. Looking across Mudge Pond toward the next hilltop reveals Skip and Judy Barber's house, which Sam also designed.

WITH PEN AND MIKE

Writing seems to come easily for someone as articulate as Posey. He briefly acquired a pop-star quality in the late '60s. *LIFE* magazine profiled him as an eligible bachelor and race driver with the long, dark sideburns de rigueur to the era in a feature story that appeared in May 1969.

On the other side of the reporters' notebook Posey also began writing for *Road & Track* in 1969. His name has appeared on the masthead for nearly 40 years as a regular contributing editor and he is referred to fondly as "Our Man Posey." He has written every manner of story for *Road & Track* but his annual selection of the Top 10 Drivers in Formula One is a reader favorite.

His aforementioned autobiography was published in 1976. The oil hadn't even cooled yet on his career. He and John Whitman retreated to a quiet place where they could piece together the early, formative events of the gravity racers, the Mudge Pond Express, the bike record and their introduction to auto racing, where Posey first topped his rival and lifelong friend. With "The Mudge Pond Express" Posey established himself as a thoughtful, articulate writer and a significant spokesman for the sport.

In "Playing with Trains: a Passion Beyond Scale" published in 2004, Sam applied himself to a new subject, building a model railroad layout for John. In typical fash-

Above: Canadian-American Challenge Cup Series, Mexico City 1968. Ray Caldwell (left) and Posey (in car) with the Caldwell D 7. Below: With John Surtees at Watkins Glen in 1972. "Surtees has not changed at all in the last 30 years."

he ever had in racing, and a crewman. The race was finally stopped – again – by rain after only 332 miles.

Neither he nor his team owner had any heart for the 1974 race. ABC Sports asked him to join the broadcast team when Jackie Stewart was scheduled to cover the Monaco Grand Prix on the same day. Posey tried it, and he liked it. He was a natural. Although his thoughtful, articulate style was dramatically opposed to Bobby Unser's excited, impatient commentary it was also easy to make fun of occasionally. Posey simply wasn't from the middle of America.

He didn't need to be. He brought his incisive, articulate point of view to the race and ABC offered him other assignments. He covered the Tour de France bicycle race, the Iditarod sled dog race in Alaska and the Iron Man Triathalon. He worked with broadcast professionals like Jim McKay and Jack Whitacre. "We always wrote our own stuff," Posey said. "And I found myself really attracted to that kind of writing—matching words to images. It's a completely different kind of writing, very simple, concise because you're competing with the images."

In 1990 he won an Emmy for the Best Writing in Sports on television.

He went on to introduce the first broadcast aired by the new Speedvision, now the SPEED channel. He continued broadcasting for over 25 years until, in one of his very few concessions to Parkinson's disease, he put down the microphone. He still writes and records Formula One promotional teasers for SPEED.

ion, the project proceeded from a clean canvas. Fifteen years later, the layout was complete after the uncontrolled forces of space, perspective, unfamiliar materials and new skills were managed to an ordered resolution.

Posey also made a seemingly effortless transition from driving and writing about racing to talking to a television audience. Posey joined ABC Sports for the Indianapolis 500 in 1974. After his hugely successful rookie debut at the Speedway in 1972, the 1973 race had been a bitter disappointment with Posey being the last driver bumped from the field. The race turned nightmarish, dragging out over three rainy, muddy days, with a horrifying crash that badly burned driver Salt Walther on the first start and another accident on the third day. That accident took the lives of driver Swede Savage, who Posey describes as one of the best friends

Top: Posey won several Emmy awards with ABC Sports. He won an individual Emmy for the Best Writing in Sports on television in 1990. Above: John Whitman originated elaborate timing techniques. Here he is timing for Sam, Jim Haines and Harry Theodoracopulous, driving Posey's Porsche 904 at Daytona in 1966.

Above: Posey was the only driver to compete for Chevrolet, Ford and Dodge in the Trans-Am series. Here he's in Roger Penske's Camaro. Below: SCCA Formula 5000, Laguna Seca 1971. "We can forget about this one, "Posey noted. "That's Hobbs ahead. Surely I must be about to lap him."

A day with Sam Posey is a day in the funhouse. It could begin – or end – with virtually anything. "I've been very fortunate," he said modestly. "That is exactly what life is like here. Anything can happen. A 'Battleships' painting. A call to Phil Hill. A question from a construction site."

"Paul Newman's grandchildren were here," Ellen quipped, "and one said, 'I know what you do for work – you play!'"

The family's two dogs choose that moment to walk in from the porch and vie for attention: identical Norwich terriers separated by 14 years, Zoe and Vodka. We've been poring over the exquisite details of Posey's new-

Left: Posey's Colorado Midland Railroad began as a simple layout for his son, John. The project took 15 years to complete. Right: The Start-Finish Tower at Lime Rock Park is typical of his simple, gracious architecture. The tower was designed with his brother David in 1990.

est diecast acquisition, a Maserati Birdcage Tipo 61. Postcards of unusual Shay-type steam locomotives are on the table. Upstairs, two large wooden constructions sit atop frames like engine stands, looking as if they have flown straight out of *"Star Wars"*. The first is called, in fact, MILLENIUM CRUISER. It is one of 12 fanciful racing machines Sam dreamed up for a tongue-in-cheek calendar created for friends. A second calendar features "Machinery for Farm and Estate" such as THE ACHILLEAN, designed to be used in the unfortunate event that "there may occur, at the far reaches of the property, unrest among workers who are not acquainted firsthand with the owner's fairness and largess." Hear, hear.

Ellen is also a talented artist. As a lark, she designed the original labels for friend Newman's salad dressing. Among her current undertakings is one called the American Mural Project. The project is described simply as an artist's tribute to the builders of America. The "tribute" will be finished as a three-dimensional mural measuring 125 feet across and nearly 50 feet high. In order to complete and display the finished piece, a foundation has been created with Paul Newman as chairman and an unused brick mill building has been purchased in Winsted, Conn. Sam says it is Ellen's accomplishment; he has helped with proposals and designed the space for the installation, connecting two long narrow buildings – one for the mural and one for

a visitors' center – with a glass atrium.

Daughter Judy has also studied at the Rhode Island School of Design and works with a producer of fashion shows in the city. Son John is working on a novel.

Houseguests are given a genuine insight into how well loved Sam and Ellen are by their friends. When the house was being built, Ellen sent out boxes to a number of friends. In each box were a few ceramic tiles, some paints and a note. Each friend was invited to create a unique design and return the tiles to Sam and Ellen. They were then fired and installed in their kitchen.

Looking around the kitchen, the visitor spots tiles created by Dan and Evi Gurney with a tiny car racing

Above: Ellen with a portion of her epic work, the American Mural Project. Collaborative projects in all 50 states are estimated to include 10,000 participants when the mural is completed. Right: Sam Posey at the home he designed for his family on the hilltop overlooking Mudge Pond.

across them. Others were designed by Jackie Stewart, Paul Newman, Chris Economaki, Frank Stella and many other friends. Each is unique and reflects the personality of the creator. Then there is one tile that enigmatically contains only the name, Phil Hill. Hill's wife, Alma, says it took him months to create. Sam reminds us that Denise McCluggage first wrote about Phil Hill in *Automobile Quarterly* (Vol. 1, No. 1) as "Hamlet in a Helmet", and we laugh. Again. AQ

The Thirty and General Motors

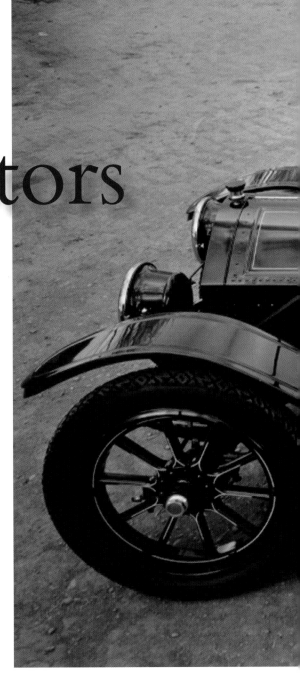

Changes and trends at Cadillac both mirrored and influenced the American auto industry in 1908. It was about this time that Henry Leland imported the first "Jo-block" gauges from Sweden for use in the Cadillac factory. The use of these famous gauges dates from the introduction of a pilot set in the Cadillac factory years before they were generally available and when expert opinion was openly skeptical. These and other technological advances came into play in the development of one of Cadillac's milestone cars, the Thirty.

BY MAURICE D. HENDRY
Excerpted From "CADILLAC: STANDARD OF THE WORLD"

1913 Model Thirty roadster.

The year 1908 was a momentous one for the American automobile in many ways. From a position behind Germany and France (but well ahead of Britain and Italy), the United States had become the foremost automobile producer in the world. In 1896, the only organized American output was 13 cars built by Duryea, but by 1900 annual production was 4,192, doubling the following year. By 1904 there were 70 establishments in the United States making and dealing in automobiles, with a capital of $20 million. A total of 24,419 cars were built that year, valued at about $45 million. Of these, cars valued at $2,695,655 were exported, more than half to British territories. Even this was merely a beginning, for 1908 saw the introduction of the Model T Ford and the incorporation of General Motors.

Imports from Europe had grown from 26 cars, valued at $43,126 in 1901 to 423 in 1904, valued at $1,466,303. French primacy among European makes was shown by the breakdown: 368 cars were French, 22 German, 15 British, and 13 Italian—seven times as many French cars as the rest put together. Imports increased up to 1909, when 1,624 European cars valued at $2,905,000 came into the country, but shortly afterward there was a decline, for by this time the American buyer could get anything he wanted from domestic factories, whether a Model T Ford, a Mercer raceabout or a $7,000 Pierce-Arrow limousine.

Symbolizing the new stature of the American industry were the New York-to-Paris victory by the Thomas, the Vanderbilt Cup win by Locomobile and the Dewar Trophy award to Cadillac. Of the three, the third was the most significant, for the round-the-world event had little practical meaning while the occasional big motor race win by American cars hardly reflected the international status of the nation's industry. Nevertheless, all three enhanced the American image, and there was even some reflected glory in the 1909 Dewar Trophy. Although it went to the English Daimler firm for pioneering sleeve valves, everybody knew that the man behind the development was an American—Charles Y. Knight.

Opposite: The Thirty's interior. Right: A Cadillac workman testing the "Go-Not-Go" gauges. Above: The Cadillac advertising department taking appropriate advantage of the company's manufacturing standards in promoting the Thirty.

The adoption of the Johansson gauges—then unique to Cadillac—the halo of the Dewar Trophy, and the success of standardized manufacture called for something special in advertising: a commercial war cry that would epitomize it all, and fix it readily in the public mind. Lengthy paragraphs, full of qualifying phrases, however well written, would not do. Something short and pungent was needed. Fortunately someone came up with the ideal answer. In 1908, along with the new Cadillac script, company publicity began promoting the slogan "Standard of the World." Catalogues, advertisements, and even hubcaps of the cars carried it. It was not new, and did not originate at Cadillac, but it has undeniably

been made Cadillac's own. It may have been suggested by Leland's association years before with Brown and Sharpe who advertised the "World's Standard of Accuracy," while De Dion actually used the identical phrase in at least one early advertisement.

It can be criticized as a sweeping generalization, and for arrogance, hauteur or conceit—call it what you will—it has been equaled only by a few other marque slogans, but it is one that survives today.

Some cars of similar class, such as Lincoln and Mercedes-Benz, take the other view and avoid the issue—or imply that they are so good and famous that no slogan is necessary.

However, this is a negative approach. The Cadillac slogan is positive, brief, uncompromising—and catchy. All these make it an ideal "image" tool, and even today, almost 100 years later, no one has been able to come up with a superior replacement.

By contrast, models were constantly superseded. In 1908 the company introduced a new four-cylinder chassis that succeeded both the single and all previous fours, and was the only production car of the 1909

program. The sales of D, G, H and L models had been normal for their price class—around 150 units in 1905, increasing to about 250 in 1906 and 1907, and 500 in 1908. These were satisfactory figures comparable with those for the single-cylinder. Yet that model was now outmoded and its sales steeply dropping. The country was in a business slump. Cadillac employment was down to 650 men—half its normal workforce. The company balance sheets were so discouraging that Lemuel Bowen mournfully predicted bankruptcy. No dividends had been declared for 1905 and 1906 because the increasing demands for the single had dictated constant plant expansion. Since Leland invariably insisted on the best and the most up-to-date machinery, expenditure had been heavy. The company had borrowed on short-term bank credits, paying the loans off within the year from seasonal sales. A new car was necessary if Cadillac was to keep its substantial following and pay its debts. The writing on the wall was clear by June 1907, and in that month H.M. and his engineers had begun design work on the new model, the Cadillac Thirty.

Design-wise, the new car was a consolidation of existing experience rather than a step out onto fresh ground. But its commercial success far outstripped any previous Cadillac. It was deliberately planned to meet the needs of a clientele whose requirements had outgrown the single. Its potential market was gauged by Wilfred Leland, and he drew up a schedule of supplies, production and sales that carried Cadillac through the lean year of its gestation period and kept loan repayments flowing.

When the Cadillac Thirty was announced in August 1908, it was a combination of the best selling points of the two main lines that preceded it. It had the luxury and performance of the fours and the moderate price of the single. Its engine and transmission were substantially that of the previous Model G, which meant that

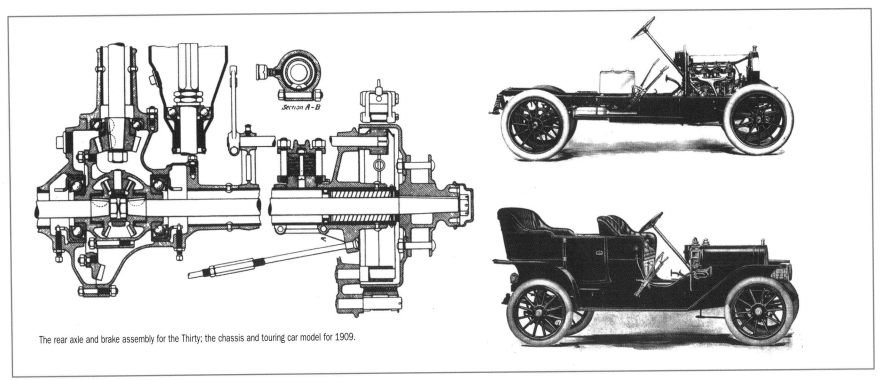

The rear axle and brake assembly for the Thirty; the chassis and touring car model for 1909.

no more Cadillacs were being built with a planetary gearset. Doubtless many followers were disappointed at the complete abandonment of planetary transmission in favor the selective sliding gear (used first on the Model G introduced for 1907). But it was simpler and more robust than the three-speed planetary, easier to service, and cheaper to make, and was now more widely accepted in America than it had been five years earlier. So, despite its driving convenience, the planetary gear had to go. (To emphasize the change, the new Thirty's pedals were clearly marked "clutch" and "brake" on the pedal pads themselves.)

The chassis was freshly designed, with platform rear suspension in place of the earlier full-elliptics, and wheelbase increased to 106 inches—six inches more than the Model G and greater than any previous Cadillac, with the exception, that is, of the 110-inch limousine of 1906. This had been priced at $5,000 – "without lamps."

In contrast, the Thirty, including full four-passenger bodywork and three oil lamps and horn, was only $1,400. Its design had been simplified, but its standard of manufacture was in one way inferior to its predecessors. How then had such a price reduction been achieved?

As opposed to the three "P's" – Packard, Peerless, Pierce-Arrow – and others who ran several models and seldom built more than a few hundred of each, Cadillac had rationalized to one chassis, and on that chassis they offered only three body styles. Every aspect of manufacturing cost had been studied, and the profit margin set at a mere $25 per car. This was only possible because the company made an unusually large proportion of the car in its own shops. It operated its own iron and brass foundries, pattern shops, sheet metal shops, machine shops, gear-cutting plant, and painting, finishing, and upholstering departments. It made its own motors, transmissions, radiators, hoods and fenders, and even its own cap screws, bolts and nuts. Its own toolmaking department designed and

made most of the 16,000 special tools, jigs, dies and fixtures used in the plant. (Standard tools and equipment totaled an additional 74,000 items.)

With a factory largely self-contained and buying its supplies in bulk at much lower rates, it was easier to control costs, maintain quality, and yet offer such exceptional value for the money. The payoff came in instant public acceptance of the Thirty and record sales in the first year. In the first six months sales at 4,500 units surpassed the previous best year, and the annual output of 5,900 cars was sold before the end of the season in August 1909. That year the directors declared a 45-percent dividend to the stockholders.

Production of the Thirty followed the principles of the earlier Cadillac models, although extra tooling was installed. "The Cadillac plant in the matter of fine machinery, fine tools, jigs and fixtures is not equaled in any other motor car factory in the world," claimed the company. "This equipment includes more than 500 special automatic labor-saving machines, some of which are capable of turning out from two to ten times the volume of work produced by the ordinary methods which obtain in most factories—and doing it far better." Methods were constantly improved, and in 1909 alone 10,000 new tools, jigs and dies were added, of which over 3,000 were designed and built by the company's own toolmaking department. "The expense for tool maintenance alone has exceeded $60,000 in a year," said one booklet.

The system of inspection was so exacting, said the factory, "that it practically precludes the possibility of an imperfect part being incorporated in the car so far as can be detected by the most accurate measuring instruments known to engineering science. … From the time the raw materials reach the warehouse until they leave the plant, they are under the careful scrutiny of the corps of experts trained in accordance with the high standards of the Cadillac organization. This inspection extends to the smallest pieces, even nuts, bolts and screws."

Suppliers found these statements true, sometimes even at their own cost. One manufacturer of grease cups who lost a contract, inquired why, and was told too many of his were substandard. To his amazement

he found that every single grease cup he supplied had to pass thread gauge and other tests.

Assembling was divided between several gangs, each assigned to particular work. One group after finishing crankshaft bearings installed the crankshaft in the motor and ran it in with a belt on the flywheel. Another group assembled the camshaft and its drive. Another assembled the cylinder, cylinder head, and copper water jacket. Final assembly was done on stands. Methods were more elaborate than with the single-cylinder model, where whole motors were assembled with only two men per stand, but subdivision of labor had not gone far, and the line was stationary. (Even at Ford, the moving line was still some years away.)

After the completed chassis had been inspected, it was placed on a roller dynamometer where final adjustments and a power check were made. The 1909 models, with four-inch bore, were rated at 25.6 hp, but developed an actual 30, hence the model designation. When the bore was increased to four and quarter inches for 1910, the rated horsepower was 28.9 and the actual went up to 33, but the original Thirty designation was retained.

Following dyno testing, in which the car had to pass a standard specification sheet, there was a road test. "I can remember the times when four-cylinder Cadillac chassis were tested on Grand Boulevard near Woodward Avenue," recalled one engineer. "That was a mighty long time ago! They were left on the sidewalk before the bodies were installed and the drivers with a box over the chassis drove them on the public roads. The early test drivers all used highways, and they had no compunction about doing anything they chose. Of course, this policy had to be changed later because of the increasing traffic and speeds."

To avoid production holdups, the dyno room was made big enough to take many cars at once, and a large staff of test drivers was retained. For many years engine testing was supervised by Charlie Martens.

Their own store of experience and standards being equal or superior to specialist vendors, Cadillac preferred to cut and finish all their own gears, both transmission and axle. Their foundry had a similar reputation and for years made cylinder, piston and piston ring castings "for a number of other automobile manufacturers making the highest priced cars in America." Although they mentioned no names, it is

A plan view of the Thirty chassis, as depicted in a 1909 brochure.

known that one was Pierce-Arrow.

The selection of materials was given as much attention as the actual manufacture of the car. "Where in most cars, particularly in those selling at (the same) price, cast iron is used in many parts, we used steel drop forgings." The cylinders, pistons and piston rings were cast in Cadillac's own foundry, the grade and formula being "the result of years of experience,

1908 Cadillac Model Thirty.

experimenting and testing in our own laboratories." These statements, made in 1908 and 1909, would have stupefied many company executives who thought laboratories were only found in colleges and scientific establishments.

So much for the Thirty's research and manufacture. What was it like in service and on the road? Did it justify the claim that despite its medium price, it was "accorded a position alongside of those few cars which stand at the pinnacle of the world's esteem"? Was it

really what Cadillac claimed it to be – a "high-grade motorcar"? The answer to the first question is "highly satisfactory," and to the second and third, a loud "Yes," but the answers require more detailed explanations.

On the road the Thirty was a pleasant, easy-handling, sweet-running car. It did not equal competitors' sixes for smoothness, but the engine was as tractable, quiet and generally refined as a four could ever hope to be.

Output at about 8.3 bhp/liter was average for 1909, and gave very good torque through a limited rev range, the cars pulling well and having a good reputation as hill climbers. Three axle ratios – 3.0, 3.5, and 4.0 to 1 – were available, the 3.5 being standard on the touring, demi-tonneau, and roadster models and giving a high gear range of 5 to 50 mph. The standard limousine ratio was 4.0 to 1, this also being available on the touring, demi-tonneau and roadster. The roadster could be ordered with a 3.0-to-1 axle giving 50 mph at only 1580 rpm.

The clutch and transmission were refined. The cars rode well and had the characteristic appeal of the big four-cylinder effortlessly tugging a high-gear ratio. On restored examples, the gentle bubble of the exhaust and the high driving position give today's driver the impression he is traveling at 20-25 mph when the car is actually cruising at 40-45.

What the Thirty could do on the track when stripped was surprising. T.J. Beaudet drove a 1911 Thirty speedster into second place at a Los Angeles board track meeting 24-hour race, covering 1,448 miles at an average speed of 60.33 mph. Although in racing trim, the car had to carry lighting equipment and a riding mechanic, and its time was the best ever put up by a car of its horsepower class up to that time.

After several years of producing cars in the "luxury" price bracket, Cadillac elected to pin all on the "under $2,000" range, much of which had to do with factory reasons. Much also was based on the attitudes of the buyers. In the older centers like New York, Boston, Cleveland and Washington, there was a sufficient core of wealthy buyers to make production of the most expensive cars viable. The title of one O. Henry book, "The Four Million", shows that New York, as always, was No. 1. Detroit's population was barely 300,000. Cars such as the six-cylinder 60hp Pierce, Peerless, Thomas and Stevens-Duryea, to name a few, were well suited to the social New Yorker or Bostonian. Like the people who bought them, they were smoother, more refined, and more powerful. But they were less practical in the cities of western expansion, where the old frontier virtues of simplicity and lower running costs were better appreciated, and in fact practically mandatory. The prospect in Detroit, or in the Midwest, or on the Pacific Coast, was not particularly interested in the New Yorker's ideal automobile or even, for that matter, the Clevelander's. Conditions were different, more primitive. For this reason six-cylinder cars never had the early success in Detroit that they enjoyed in Cleveland and New York State, and even Packard sold cars in the $4,000-5,000 price range with no more than four cylinders right up to 1912.

One major shortcoming of the big sixes (successful

Right: The Thirty engine from 1909.

medium-sized sixes did not appear until the second decade) was inadequate cooling in severe conditions. Richmond Viall, Leland's old superintendent at Brown and Sharpe, bought one of the first Cadillac Thirty models, and in September 1909 he reported to Leland that during a 17-day tour he had no cooling problems, whereas a neighbor's $5,000 Peerless, traveling in company, boiled frequently. And in a private interoffice memo of July 1912, the chief engineer of Pierce-Arrow admitted that boiling problems increased with the displacement, being least on their 38 hp and most on their 66, which "almost invariably boiled in hot weather conditions."

Another big six drawback was running costs, including tire bills, which would have startled all but J. P. Morgan. The log of a 1908 Pierce Great Arrow operated by a Boston doctor for the three years 1909-1911, averaging 5,000-6,000 miles a year, shows that the annual tire bill averaged $533. Gas and oil came next at $326. For comparison at the other end of the scale, a Model T Ford operated by the same man cost $85.20 for tires and $69.15 for gas and oil. The Cadillac Thirty offered a reasonable compromise between these extremes, and combined something of the best attributes of both vehicles.

Then there was the question of sheer size. The lightest six-cylinder Pierce weighed well over 4,000 lbs, the heaviest exceeded 6,000, and their wheelbases ranged from 119-135 inches. Although the Pierces in particular were remarkably easy-handling for their size and era, cars of these proportions were generally considered to be a handful for the owner-driver and more suited to a chauffeur. And he cost even more than the tires!

Therefore (as Henry Ford had found already), few people in Detroit were in the market for a big six when the Thirty was designed. Cadillac was undoubtedly capable of building such a car, but marketing it would have probably led them straight into bankruptcy.

In answer to the second of our leading questions, then, the Cadillac Thirty was a well-chosen concept, and the car was properly designed and thoroughly tested throughout. Despite its moderate price, it was manufactured according to standards unsurpassed even in factories building cars costing several times the price. Several of them, in fact, had been shown by Leland how to build quality and precision into the product, rather than the other way around. By comparison with those of costly contemporaries, the Cadillac's specifications were modest, but a logical, practical answer to the needs of its environment. And although it conceded points in power, speed and refinement to the bigger cars, it certainly scored over them in other, equally important respects.

Pierce-Arrow catalogues of the day proclaimed that there were "three classes of car: cheap cars, cars of compromise, and cars of quality." Immediately listing their own in the third class, they remarked that cheap cars were bought because they were cheap, and compromise cars were bought because the purchaser could not afford true quality.

This was a shrewd summary, but not entirely correct. In effect, Cadillac had created a fourth category with its Thirty—a car of true quality but moderate in price and running costs. Both at the price and above,

it had few contemporaries of comparable reputation and success. One Studebaker-produced car in the same price range became known as the "Every-Mechanical-Failure." Another manufacturer, Thomas, trading on its reputation, built a car selling for twice the price and virtually ruined itself honoring the warranty of defective cars. A third, Lozier, watched its own fortunes decline for five years, then set out in 1913 to recover them with a car that used the four-cylinder Cadillac as its model.

During 1908, promoting its new six-cylinder, Pierce-Arrow generously admitted "the great and lasting merits of the four-cylinder." (The company was still making some itself.) "Well-made cars of this type," it continued, "have wonderful possibilities of motoring accomplishments, both for city use and country touring; they are most satisfying and have all the possibilities of the six, save in very slight degree." This advertisement was probably drafted by Pierce-Arrow's chief engineer David Fergusson. Some years later he was more specific, for he wrote: "Cadillac

seen more than a year's service," while later on they reported: "Recently we had occasion to examine the bearings of a car which had traveled 46,000 miles, yet the wear proved not to exceed the one-one-thousandth of an inch."

Nothing illustrates better the Thirty's longevity than some service records established under the particularly rugged conditions that existed in New Zealand. During 1911 a number of Thirties went into service with Newman Brothers, a renowned South Island coachline. Established in Nelson in 1879, the concern was making the changeover from horses to horsepower. In 1912 a Thirty made the first automobile journey from Nelson to Westport via the Buller Gorge. The same year a regular run was established

Top: The Model Thirty select type-sliding gear transmission. Above: Model Thirty Cadillacs on dynamometer test, 1913.

for years had the reputation of producing the best medium-priced car in the world."

Overseas the four-cylinder was regarded as a worthy successor to earlier models, and the English observer, F.A. Talbot, stated that by 1912 the Thirty was already "an old favorite amongst British motorists … all the parts of this car are fashioned with precision and care … (it is) a homogeneous and silent whole."

More than 50 years later English historian Anthony Bird echoed this comment, remarking that the cars were "as refined and reliable as money could make them."

The company was therefore justified in saying that the Cadillac Thirty needed no fancy price tag to bolster its claim to be a car of world class, and they harped on it at every opportunity. They were unperturbed by the European propaganda campaign directed against the rising menace of the American automobile. In fact they met this criticism head on.

In service the cars were building up a fine reputation for durability and reliability. During 1910 the factory commented that "we have yet to hear of the first broken crankshaft although a vast number of cars have

and the cars made the round trip three times a week. "Motor Mail Coach" conversions were made, the chassis being lengthened and special bodies installed with extra rows of seats. This included a return to the old rear-tonneau-entrance style, but with a total load of 10 passengers. Sometimes up to 16 passengers were carried, with scores of mailbags and luggage. With luggage loaded on first – along running boards, between hood and guards, and even on top of the hood – the driver sometimes had to sit on top of parcels to get a clear view of the road. Passengers above the normal

1909 Cadillac Model Thirty

load had to sit on mudguards, on the luggage, and at the back on the folded top.

Rough roads, steep climbs and frequent river crossings were normal; the cars were specially prepared for these river crossings, as they were sometimes all but submerged. Portable windlasses known as "pull-me-outs" were carried for hauling out stranded cars. Reliability,

long life and low running costs were paramount, for the timetable was public, and the company private. The thrice-weekly round trip totaled 900 miles, or approximately 46,000 miles per year. In service for 12 years, each car clocked up more than half a million miles.

BEHIND THE SCENES

It is worthwhile at this point to review behind-the-scenes developments within the walls of the Cadillac plant during the era of the Thirty, and particularly to study the two Lelands, father and son, who were the major personalities.

The morale among the workforce was high. Leland

41

himself was regarded with admiration and affection by his close associates, with respect by responsible workmen, and with awe by the juniors and apprentices. To the latter he was a legendary figure whose experience seemed to stretch back almost to the beginnings of the machine age, certainly before many of them had been born. Though of an age when most men reserve their energy – or what is left of it – for retirement, hobbies and grandchildren, he had the mental alertness and physical fitness of men 20 years younger in the prime of their careers. His endurance earned the respect of the toughest men on his payroll, as did his manual skill. Managing the great industrial organization which he had sustained in a new and increasingly competitive field, he could still enter any shop in the factory and produce work at the bench equal or superior to that done by the best employees. Even in his 70s, although his hearing was poor as it always had been, and he constantly had to wear spectacles, "his hands were still drawn to steel and machinery as if by a magnet," and his sharp eyes could still read off the graduations on a micrometer barrel and detect the slightest variation. It was said he was "never seen without a micrometer in his hand." This, of course, is a figure of speech, but it is likely he carried one in his pocket and often used it. One celebrated instance was the occasion when he

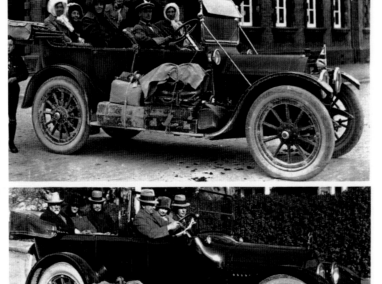

Top: A quartet of Cadillacs in the Newman Service, outside the post office in Nelson, New Zealand, before embarking cross country, circa 1918. Above: Newman Service Cadillacs.

demonstrated to Alfred P. Sloan that Hyatt bearings, which the latter was selling, were inaccurately made. Sloan, then a young graduate engineer of about 30, had to sit humbly in Leland's office watching the old man's beard wag at him as he emphasized the importance of

sticking to tolerance.

In "Adventures of a White Collar Man", Sloan described the incident: "Under Mr. Leland's brown hand with it broad thumb was a micrometer. He had measured the diameters of several specimen bearings. Then he had drawn lines and written down the variations from the agreed tolerances. … We discussed interchangeability of parts. A genuine conception of what mass production should mean really grew in me with that conversation."

Physically H.M. was a big man – over six feet tall, and broad-shouldered. "In his rugged, masterful strength few men could measure up to him," wrote his secretary John Bourne. "Only by his silvered hair would one think of the ripening of time. Nothing of age was suggested by his voice or manner. Vigor characterized all that he did. His skin was fresh, his eyes twinkled. He walked and talked and thought rapidly."

Intensely human, Leland liked to mix with men and be one of them. He played no golf or other sports, but was the family champion at dominoes and lawn bowls, and occasionally a ball game appealed to him. He liked hearing and telling good, clean stories, had a nimble wit and a soul-satisfying laugh. Although a teetotaler and nonsmoker, he could sit serene and unannoyed through long meetings in dense tobacco smoke, though needless to say, these meetings were outside his own plant.

But H.M. was also a good hater. He always "carried his backbone around," and knew when and how to be severe. Always intolerant of blundering, carelessness and indifferent workmanship and thinking, he possessed the biblical hatred for some things, and his frown was "bleak as winter."

"When he opened the floodgates of his wrath," wrote John Bourne, "he swept up everything pertaining and poured it out in caustic denunciation," while L.D. Burlingam tut-tutted, "In spite of Leland's strong religious background and high ideals, he is somewhat free in using strong lanuage and telling experiences of his life where such language has been applied."

Yet he was essentially a kind and gentle man, constantly visiting hospitals, giving to charities (sometimes as much as a third or even half his annual salary), paying the mortgage of an employee's widow, holding up businessmen while discussing the hopes and troubles of one of his shopmen. He even bailed an old bum out of jail, saying, "How would you like to spend the night in jail if you were 80 and had no friends?"

Leland worked on the principle that one should make it difficult for people to do things the wrong way. "He used to say that he would fire any man who had a file at his bench," said Le Roi J. Williams. "The parts had to be made so that they didn't require any file, and H.M. wouldn't tolerate the manufacture of any parts that had any burs or sharp points that a workman could cut his finger on."

"H.M. wasn't impressed by theories," continued Williams. "He was an apostle of direct experiment and in finding out whether or not things worked you must demonstrate their success. H.M. was one of the first to propose putting untried new models on the road for 24 hours, grueling road tests with cars loaded with sandbags and subjected to treatment and road conditions far beyond normal."

H.M. could be cryptic, as during the awarding of the Dewar Trophy in London when he was asked how Cadillac was able to manufacture cars with interchangeable parts. Williams recalled he answered that "it was a rather simple process, that you first of all had

1913 Model Thirty Touring

to know what you were going to do, and second you had to know how you wanted to do it, and thirdly you had to do it that way."

And he could be brutally blunt on the same subject, noting on another occasion, without mentioning names, that "I was in an assembly room once four times as large as the assembly room I had at the Cadillac factory, and they had five times as many people because 'they had fitters.' Fitters everywhere, and so many turned out 15 engines when I was turning out 100. Five times as many men; four times as much room and it was all due to poor tolerances. … Don't bother with fitters – you should get along without fitters. That is the trouble with the whole of Europe today; labor is cheap – they make the parts and give them to fitters to fit together."

On "running-in" engines, Leland was equally scathing: "They don't know what their limits are. They said they run it with a belt for 10 hours and then run it on its own power for 30 hours. Now I never started an engine on anything but its own power."

H.M. was always interested in the welfare of his workmen, whom he continued to call "his boys" even when they had served with him for several decades. "I still call them boys," he said on one occasion, "because they were not really much more than that when they came to us 20 years ago."

Plant conditions in the early days were primitive. Charlie Martens recalled, "We had no washrooms or lockers, no cafeterias, no canteens, no gum machines. We used to put our clothes on a long pole and hang them way up on a wall or post. We did have a medical department … sort of. [It] had a nurse and doctor."

The plain fact was that in the early days the company could not afford "luxuries," nor was it a period of workmen's amenities, smoking rooms and the like. However, as the company prospered, conditions improved.

Leland was autocratic about some things – particularly liquor and tobacco – to an extent that would bring a plant out on strike today. "His moral concepts tolerated no compromise," recalled Ernest W. Seaholm. "Thus if caught smoking on the premises the penalty was a summary discharge."

In time, however, apparently influenced by the milder-tempered Wilfred, Leland's attitude in these areas became more flexible. Although intolerant of sloppy work, Leland was warm in his praise of a job well done. His reaction to the winning of the Dewar Trophy was typical. When the cup itself, a magnificent piece of silverwork of very high value, was sent over from England complete with engraved baseplate, Leland had it displayed in the factory for all to see. Each workman was given a small leaflet describing the test, with H.M.'s personal congratulations for making its success possible—the handshaking involved about a thousand men and Leland told them, "The honor belongs equally to every honest, sincere and conscientious member of this organization, no matter what his position."

"That was a day!" recalled Charlie Martens. "Everybody felt mighty proud when Mr. Leland displayed the trophy in the lobby."

Both Lelands were, according to members of the family, "typical New Englanders, who were practical men literally to their fingertips, yet appreciative of finer culture." Both had traveled widely and Wilfred had been to Europe as early as 1896. Both kept thoroughbred horses and Henry enjoyed riding

The equestrian Henry Leland, 1910.

even when he was approaching 70. Both were great readers and lovers of classical literature. The elder Leland remembered few quotations, although he liked to quote Macaulay's Horatius. Wilfred, however, had a prodigious memory in this regard, and his widow, Ottilie Leland, told this writer: "Wilfred had a memory that even Henry Ford admired, saying, 'Wilfred had the figures at his fingertips.' He never used notes. He had a photographic mind. He could stand at a gift shop window and read a poem on a card, and then turn and repeat it to me. I was always amazed. He could recite 150 poems and was asked to recite at many parties— long, humorous ones, or long epics, or tiny gems about a brook or a flower. He was a charming speaker, like his father, although less forceful. He was a real gentleman

of the old New England school in thought and manner, as was his father."

Both Lelands were public-spirited men too, and H.M. was as well known in local politics as he was in the engineering world. Both community interest and Cadillac's interest benefited from one Leland project: the founding by H.M. in 1907 of the Cadillac School of Applied Mechanics. The growth of the industry was outstripping the supply of machinists, technicians and toolmakers, and this was his answer. It was the first such school in the automobile industry and was another of the many ways in which he influenced the industrial development of his country. Trainees were given two years' grounding in all phases of machine work, automobile design and assembly, drafting, mathematics and metallurgy. An additoinal year on an advanced course was available (bringing the total hours of instruction to 9,000) provided the pupil continued with Cadillac for a further two years. Characteristically, Leland laid down as requirement No. 1: "Students must be of good moral character."

While most of the graduates continued to work for Cadillac, others went to the Dodge Brothers, Hudson Motors, Studebaker Corporation, Ford and numerous machine shops in the Detroit area. The school's success was followed by the founding, nine years later, of the Ford Trade School, organized by S.E. Wilson, who had been an instructor at the Cadillac school. From then onward other major manufacturers adopted the idea.

Shortly after the Thirty was announced in 1908, a representative of General Motors, Arnold Goss, had called on the stockholders of Cadillac. He had been sent by William Crapo Durant to make an offer for the company. Durant, born in 1860, was an automotive Napoleon. In 1904 he bought and reorganized the Buick Motor Company. After an unsuccessful attempt to merge Buick, Maxwell-Briscoe, Ford and Reo in

1908, he organized a new corporation in New York on Sept, 16, 1908. Charles Eaton was the first president, Buick was its initial substance, and the incorporation involved no more than $2,000. The company was known as General Motors.

Durant's aim was to combine into one large industrial organization a variety of makes covering the market from top to bottom, together with the associated suppliers of all components and accessories. Although this in principle, to some extent, had already been put into practice – unsuccessfully – by the Pope organization, it was a remarkably farsighted view for 1908, anticipating much of the corporate development of later decades. Durant, however, had some serious personal weaknesses, summarized by Alfred Sloan as "the ability to create but not administer." These were to bring trouble within a few years. In 1908, however, he was riding high.

Already in control of Buick, Durant next acquired Oldsmobile, then turned his eyes on Cadillac. He wanted Cadillac first because it was a very sound company promising profitable operation and secondly because it produced a car of superior quality.

Provided they could show a profit, the major stockholders at Cadillac were interested in selling out, for their experience in the new automobile business had been hectic, strange and anxious. Naming Wilfred Leland as negotiator, they set a price of $3.5 million. After consultation with Durant, Goss returned the next day with a bid for $3 million. Wilfred stuck to his price and insisted on cash. Since Durant operated on equities and stock issues, he was unable to find the money and the deal fell through.

Six months later, however, Goss returned to reopen negotiations. By now, with the aura of the Dewar Trophy adding to the standing of the company, and sales of the Thirty surpassing all previous figures and bringing substantial profits, the stockholders instructed Wilfred to up the price to $4,125,000, and limit the offer to 10 days.

For the second time Durant had to let the option pass. However, Goss again returned – this time Wilfred met him with a figure of $4.5 million. By now delays

The sumptuous interior of the 1913 Model Thirty limousine.

had already cost Durant a million dollars, and had brought him no nearer control, so he reputedly accepted the Leland quotation: "Cash on the line within 10 days." It was Buick who had to foot the bill. The full purchase price, actually $5,669,250, was paid for by Buick in return for GM preferred stock to the value of $5,169,200, only the remaining $500,000 being cash. The transfer went through on July 29, 1909, and it was the largest financial transaction that had occurred on the Detroit stock exchange up to that time.

In the transfer papers the net value of the whole organization was assessed at $2,868,709. The remaining $1.8 million represented the good will built up by a company that Arthur Pound sums up as "well managed, highly prosperous, financially conservative and of unquestioned eminence in the automobile world." Far from paying too high a price, Durant had a bargain buy. Although the company was capitalized at $1.5 million, well over a million had simply been plowing back of profits. Only $327,000 in cash had gone into the company. The report of Aug. 1909, listed net

earnings for the year as $1,969,382. Three dividends totaling $45 had been paid separately in May and June 1909, and the stockholders received $300 per share on the sale of stock.

"Actually the company was a tremendous bargain which only William Durant appreciated," comment Henry Leland's biographers. "A concern that earned almost two million a year was not overpriced at four and a half million."

Since Cadillac continued to earn at this rate and above for the next 10 months, returning to General Motors an additional $2 million, Durant had every reason to feel pleased with himself. And in addition, he had obtained the continuing services of the men who had made such earnings possible. The latter, however, had not been possible without a further concession by Durant.

Immediately after the transaction had taken place, Durant had called the Lelands to the Russell House in Detroit, where he was staying, and asked them to continue as managers of Cadillac. The Leland reply was that their standards and principles mattered more to them than any other consideration. If they could continue to run the company as they had in the past, all would be well, but if their ideas were going to be compromised they wanted no part of it.

Durant readily nodded his assent, saying, "That is exactly what I want. I want you to continue to run Cadillac exactly as though it were your own. You will receive no directions from anyone."

Thus, having sold Cadillac on their own terms, the Lelands returned to it, again on their own terms. The advantages of membership in General Motors, an assured market position in their chosen field, mutual benefits with associated companies all were to become obvious to Cadillac in later years. But at the time there were more problems than benefits.

For all his business flair, salesmanship and confidence, Durant moved too far and too fast. He was temperamentally a gambler and acquired too many companies too soon. This required overcapitalization, and Durant and General Motors were soon at the mercy of the bankers. When loans were called, some constituent companies proved worthless and the others could not earn sufficient income to carry their debts. Buick, for instance, in 1910 owed $7 million to the First Bank of Boston, and Durant's bank loans as a whole had been overextended by about $12 million. Cadillac's part in this period deserves some comment.

Since Buick had been the cornerstone of GM, the bankers were in favor of rescuing Buick, if possible, and winding up General Motors if necessary. However, they reckoned without Wilfred Leland. He was usually content in his father's shadow, but at this critical time the elder Leland, reassured by Durant that banks would come through with the necessary credit, had gone overseas for a tour of the automobile plants on the Continent. Wilfred decided to take a firm stand on his own.

Twenty-two bankers had assembled in the Chase National Bank in New York in September 1910, and had agreed that they would neither grant any new loans nor extend any existing loans to General Motors for a single day. They had lost faith in both Durant and his corporation. And they questioned the treasurer of Cadillac closely about his company's affairs. Wilfred remonstrated with them vigorously. "Father was in Europe," he said later, "and I did my best to save his reputation and our company."

That afternoon the bankers appointed a committee for the purpose of deciding whether to dissolve General Motors. It met that evening at 8:00 in the old Belmont Hotel. Wilfred's spirited performance earlier that day had impressed the bankers, and he was invited to present his case for GM to the committee that night.

For several hours the younger Leland argued with the group of hard-headed financiers who had already made up their minds to cut their losses. Quietly he recounted the triumphs of Cadillac, technical and financial, its secure position and reputation – now worldwide – the integrity and genius of his father, and the determination and ability of the Leland organization to imbue the whole of General Motors Corporation with similar success, provided they were given the opportunity. He had no doubt that the bankers' investment would be retrieved and large profits made within a few years.

The committee chairman, a Chicago banker named Ralph van Vechten, was the first to be convinced, and by 2:30 a.m. Wilfred Leland had won the rest over.

However, because the bankers distrusted Durant, the terms were stiff. General Motors received $12 million in cash, but had to repay $15 million at 6-percent interest, the bankers took $6 million in General Motors' stock, and Durant was compelled to withdraw from active management. He was to return again dramatically five years later.

Cadillac test cars and drivers.

James J. Storrow of Boston succeeded Durant as president of General Motors and was followed by Thomas Neal, a Detroit businessman. These men vigorously overhauled the corporation's finance and organization, leaning heavily on Wilfred Leland. Henry Leland, on his return from Europe, went through the engineering side of GM, raising efficiency and standards. In H.M.'s office, either the old man or a deputy was always on call, 24 hours a day.

In the rebuilding process, the Lelands imparted to the other GM units their methods and techniques, either personally or through their key associates. H.M.'s foundry superintendent, Joe Wilson, sorted out Buick's foundry problems, while his factory superintendent, Walter Phipps, advised Oakland and Buick on production. Ernest Sweet, Leland's most capable engineer, made frequent trips through the other companies, advising, guiding and reporting back to Henry. Charles Oostdyke, Wilfred's purchasing agent at Cadillac, was appointed purchasing agent over all GM divisions. Henry Leland personally taught the key machinists to use precision gauges and instructed them in inspection and testing methods. Charles Nash and Walter Chrysler, then at Buick but later to found their own companies, spent weekends at the Leland country home discussing manufacturing problems. H.M. even visited the Fisher Body Plant, recommended a change to metal-paneled bodies and other improvements, and placed an unheard-of order for 150 units to start off quantity production of closed bodies, a new development in this field. Thus General Motors was carried through its most critical period on the shoulders of Buick with Cadillac as the "head."

Since Alfred P. Sloan has stated that Buick and Cadillac were the "substance" of the original General Motors, and since Cadillac was the only solvent member of the corporation, had probably the best management and certainly the finest engineers, it is clear that Cadillac's role was decisive. This corporate achievement, hard on the technical triumphs of 1908, would have provided sufficient laurels for most companies, but Cadillac engineers were already preparing for other far-reaching mechanical advancements.

1916 Series 53 touring. After the Thirty came the series 51 in 1915, then the 53 in 1916. That year, more than 18,000 V-8-powered Series 53 models sold.

PATCH COLLECTION

BY TRACY POWELL

Nostalgia means different things to different people. Most settle for the warm feelings associated with good memories, usually from childhood and always fleeting – real life soon sets in after the moment of remembrance has passed. Not so for Glenn Patch. Patch opts to live in the past, and he loves every minute of it.

Graduating from high school in Picayune, Miss., in 1959, Patch's classic car collection has allowed him to attend a perpetual high school reunion. He never outgrew his pursuit for all things '50s, a passion that has traveled with him through his successful years in the worlds of publishing and real estate development.

Patch is an entrepreneur who made his way in the publishing industry with magazines such as *Shutterbug*, *Computer Shopper* and other national magazines. He successfully sold his media properties to the Ziff Davis Group after *Computer Shopper* had become the largest-circulation magazine in the IT genre.

"I've always loved the fifties, that atmosphere, and of course the cars," said Patch, the founder of GEP, Inc, the Titusville, Fla., holding company whose portfolio includes numerous real estate developments. "As a kid, you just couldn't wait for the new cars to come out, to go to the showrooms and see them. And I've wanted to collect them for some time."

Selling his magazine properties "gave me adequate cash flow" to pursue the dream of collecting, which began in earnest in the early 1990s.

"I had 48 cars from the '50s era and into the early '60s," Patch said. "After a while I began thinking that no matter how much money I spent I couldn't get them all, even if I built bigger buildings to hold them all. So then I decided I needed a goal, something to work towards. Because I graduated from high school in 1959, I thought I'd get every '59 convertible, all 100-point cars or at least as close to that as possible. I started looking at some pictures of '59 models and

there were some I didn't like. But I loved every '57. Also, when you talk to collectors of '50s cars they always say that '57 is the classic year."

Another reason for Patch to choose that year was because of the long list of automotive "firsts." Among other innovations, it was the first year for fuel injection for many makes. It was the last year for Dodge to offer its much-loved Hemi engine, as well as the last for Packard, Hudson and Nash production.

Patch researched that year's makes and found that 32 different convertible models were manufactured by American companies. At that point he decided to sell off his other cars and devote his attention to these 32 topless beauties. Examples that were as close to 100 point as possible were still desirable. One of these was a frame-up restoration, which led Patch to Wisconsin.

"That was my first '57 collectible," he said. "It was a De Soto Adventurer. I looked at it and it was gorgeous, restored perfectly. Even the record player in the

There isn't one American-made model of 1957 vintage that leaves Glenn Patch dissatisfied. Left: Buick Roadmaster convertible. Right: Taillight assembly, complete with fin, on the Buick Special.

dash worked."

The 1957 De Soto Golden Adventurer was a glimmering gem among other jewels of American offerings for that year. Leading into that year, however, production schedules had been severely cut and sales were lagging. Little was expected for American cars on the show circuit. Along with the Plymouth Fury, the Golden Adventurer, with its ultra-white paint job and gold-finished adornments, made a big splash to all those present. De Soto rolled this model out with bigger bores than before, raising the engine to 5.5 liters. With a 9.25 to 1 compression ratio, the engine produced 320 bhp, and top speed was said to reach 130 mph.

"Through the process of buying that car, I asked the owner where he had gotten it restored," Patch said. "That's how I met Bob Schmidt."

Schmidt owned a high-end restoration shop at the time in the Phoenix area. Patch flew out to meet Schmidt to check on Schmidt's availability and willingness to help locate the remaining 31 convertibles. Schmidt began sourcing soon thereafter. After about a month of search-and-find work, Schmidt told Patch, "Glenn, I like working for you and getting these cars, but you'll save a lot of money if you just bought my company. I love restoring cars but I don't like the front office." Patch took him up on the suggestion and purchased the restoration business. Schmidt has been working for Patch full-time since, about 15 years ago.

"Glenn wanted this project completed in a five-year period," Schmidt said. "At first it was going to be the 32 convertibles, but before it was all over we ended up doing 66. We still had them done within six years. We were able to do it with the help of a lot of people at swap meets and shows, a lot of word of mouth. I started the project 15 years ago, and there was no e-Bay at that time. I didn't even have a computer when I started – it would have been a big help, but a computer didn't come along until after we were finished."

Schmidt has now restored classics on a professional level for 25 years after 20 years as a hobby. He still attends car shows and swap meets, as well as antique shops and auction houses, now primarily to hunt for memorabilia.

"Once I got into this project, we had 12 and 13 frame-offs going at one time," Schmidt said. "Our body shop couldn't keep up, so Glenn used several other body shops that did the same quality work that we did. These were the types of shops that serviced cars that would go to Pebble Beach and other events. So I was crossing the United States from Seattle to Boston to Fort Lauderdale to San Diego, chasing after cars that people said were number-one cars but were far from it. Some of the cars were not as nice as we would have liked to start with."

Fortunately, with his shop in the Phoenix area at the time, Schmidt and his dozen employees had access to salvage yards populated with rust-free relics.

Left: The glamorous Cadillac Series 62. Above: Chevrolet built its Black Widow specifically to race in NASCAR. The car was based off a 1957 model 150 two-door "utility" sedan, the same sedan that Chevy sold to police fleets and the U.S. Army. The Black Widow came beefed up with a fuel-injected 283-cubic-inch V8 straight out of the Corvette that boasted 270 hp. As irony would have it, the fuel-injected 283 was the reason NASCAR outlawed the car, because it didn't have a carburetor. There were only a handful built.

have them on display, to share them with people."

Patch had purchased some land in Southern California, the plan being to open '57 Heaven along an interstate in Palm Springs. After hearing that Bob Petersen was losing money at his museum at the time because of high costs associated with doing business in Los Angeles, Patch reconsidered the location. "I thought that would take the fun out of it real quick."

AN EYE ON BRANSON

Meanwhile, Patch had also been acquiring land in and around Branson, Mo., since 1990, to today's tune of an accumulated 10,000 acres. On his land Patch has opened two golf courses and a high-end housing development, as well

Replacement panels and parts, therefore, were ideal for the project.

One of the Pontiac Bonnevilles proved a special challenge for Schmidt.

"It was really a basket case," Schmidt said. "It was rusty, probably hadn't run in 30 years or more. Each Pontiac dealer in the country got one; there were only 630 made. Therefore you didn't have much of a choice during restoration – you dealt with what you could find."

Perhaps the greatest overall challenge, however, have been most of the collection's Chrysler Group products: the Chryslers, De Sotos, Dodges, Plymouths and Imperials. Though handsomely styled, that year's models were notorious for rust and poor construction.

"When they were 2 or 3 years old their fenders were flapping in the breeze already," Schmidt said. "Those cars were a challenge in regards to the sheet metal. But again, being able to scour the salvage yards in Arizona, as well as California and even New Mexico, it was doable."

At that point, Patch was looking for something to do with his collection. The cars were kept in a building in Phoenix, a building that was sealed up due to space constraints. But Patch "thought it would be nice to

Virgil Exner's designs for 1957 were beginning to set the standard for modern design. Left: Chrysler's New Yorker. Right: The Adventurer was De Soto's high-performance entry, boasting the first standard equipment engine producing one horsepower for every cubic inch of displacement (345 hp came from 345 cubic inches at 5200rpm). It was also a head-turner in 1957. It certainly caught Patch's attention. Shown here is a hardtop; Patch also has a convertible.

as the Branson Airport, which is expected to take commercial flights in May 2009. A friend was also a real estate investor who owned five acres along Highway 76, otherwise known as The Strip in Branson because of the Vegas-style neon signs and attractions (without the casinos). That friend approached Patch to gauge his interest in opening a '50s-themed complex, namely a diner connected to a theatre. The spacious basement, plenty big enough to hold Patch's collection, was of immediate appeal to Patch. To all parties involved, the tens of thousands of cars that passed by the property each week was incentive enough to move forward.

"With everything considered, it took a lot of the risk out of opening a museum," Patch said. "I ended up buying the whole thing."

The complex's main attraction is Dick Clark's American Bandstand Theater, a 900-seat venue that hosts shows by some of the greatest musical performers from the 1950s and '60s including the Righteous Brothers, Bill Medley, Paul Revere and the Raiders, The

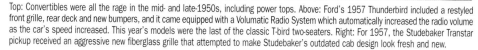
Top: Convertibles were all the rage in the mid- and late-1950s, including power tops. Above: Ford's 1957 Thunderbird included a restyled front grille, rear deck and new bumpers, and it came equipped with a Volumatic Radio System which automatically increased the radio volume as the car's speed increased. This year's models were the last of the classic T-bird two-seaters. Right: For 1957, the Studebaker Transtar pickup received an aggressive new fiberglass grille that attempted to make Studebaker's outdated cab design look fresh and new.

find a turquoise couch with clear, plastic covering, as well as a Christmas tree with presents underneath and a period kitchen.

Appreciation comes after taking in the whole package, which instantly plants visitors in the period. Think instant time travel into television's "Happy Days" set.

As he related in a speech he gave when the complex first opened, Patch is living his dream of re-living his youth – or at least that era.

"I get up in the morning, go play golf on one of my golf courses, come in here to the diner and eat lunch. Then I go see a show in the theatre and go for a walk down Main Street U.S.A. through my collection. Later I'll go upstairs and have a nightcap at the club."

"After so many years of keeping these classics to myself, moving the collection to Branson and incorporating it into the whole Dick Clark '50s experience has been incredibly gratifying."
—Glenn Patch

Above: One of the limited-production Chrysler Dual-Ghias can be found in Patch's collection. Below: The last year for Hudson production was 1957. Shown here: The Hudson Hornet Hollywood.

Comets, Gary Lewis and the Playboys, Fabian, Bobby Vee, The Chiffons, Bryan Hyland and Chris Montez. Headliners are original performers that were televised during American Bandstand's broadcasts. Dick Clark's Grill, a '50s-themed diner with Dick Clark memorabilia, is also onsite. The top floor of the complex features a bar called Club 57. Visitors can see a show, have lunch or dinner, and browse through '57 Heaven.

"I didn't want to lose the wife and the kids when dad wanted to see the collection, when most wives say, 'Oh no, not another car museum.' I've been collecting the memorabilia the last few years, too, so you've got the whole lifestyle of the '50s when you go down there."

Cars are parked amidst department stores, toy stores, a Texaco gas station, a drive-in movie theater, an ice cream parlor, and a period ranch house, all to draw in visitors and emulate a moment frozen in time. What sells the effect are the authentic "props" – Patch has ensured that nothing superficial creeps in. One example is the ranch house's interior décor. Here you'll

Branson: Center Stage

Branson, Mo., sometimes referred to as a "Family-Friendly Las Vegas," may not appear to offer much by way of world-class entertainment. Today, approximately 7,500 people are residents, by all definitions making Branson a small Midwestern town. Branson was originally envisioned as a center for lumber shipment from the Ozark Mountains, but city leaders began to develop tourism in the 1930s. It has since grown into a major regional destination with a well-known reputation for live music theaters, primarily in the country genre.

Branson hosts three major amusement parks, as well as a diversified armada of live theaters that house everything from comedy and magic shows to variety music and dancing. Built along a portion of Highway 76 nicknamed "The Strip" because of its Vegas-style roadside neon signs, Branson has indeed become the family-friendly version of its Nevada counterpart.

Tourism has its roots in author, painter and pastor Harold Bell Wright, who began visiting the area in 1898 and used it for the setting in his book "Shepherd of the Hills". Following that book's publication in 1907, the area's first tourists were spotted, fans of Wright who wished to experience the scenic Ozarks as Wright had. The outdoor production of the "Shepherd of the Hills" is still being performed and is the longest running and most performed outdoor drama in America.

Today, Branson boasts over 100 live shows in 49 theaters with a total of 57,000 seats. Other tourist attractions include museums, three lakes, 10 championship golf courses (including the two Patch owns), an IMAX Theater, a zoo, year-round festivals and events, nearby mountains and wilderness areas. Nearly 8 million people visit Branson each year. Recently, the area was once again selected as one of the top three destinations in the country for tour and travel by the National Motorcoach Network. Branson placed no. three on the Top 10 Destinations list, following Pigeon Forge and Washington, D.C., and ahead of cities that included Nashville, Chicago and New York.

Branson's popularity as an entertainment Mecca sparked a record $173.5 million in new construction permits in 2005.

Sharing the Dream

Without a doubt, Patch's favorite part of the experience is taking a stroll down a beautiful and elaborate, 32,000 sq. ft. recreation of Main Street U.S.A. (Although taking in the shows comes in a very close second.) The lifestyle exhibit was created around '57 Heaven, which opened to the public in April 2006. The collection includes 1957 models from every American manufacturer, including Hudson, Ford, Cadillac, Buick, Chevrolet, Pontiac, Chrysler, Oldsmobile, Plymouth, Studebaker, Packard, Nash, and of course De Soto. There are nearly 60 automobiles and countless pieces of memorabilia.

"'57 Heaven is incredible, like no other I have seen before," said Dennis Gage, television host for "My Classic Car."

Automobiles rotate in and out of the collection to keep the displays fresh.

"We've not had one person go through that didn't love it," Patch said. "One guy came through last week who is a national judge for a car club, and they had been traveling from California all through the United States seeing different museums and collections. He said that ours was the finest collection they had ever seen."

In addition to production models, rare examples such as an El Morocco and the Chrysler Dual–Ghia are on display. Visitors will find a Ford that was owned by "Fireball" Roberts, and a Pontiac that once set the world's stock car race record at 141.2 mph. In Patch's and Schmidt's quest to show near-perfect models, the collection includes the only Corvette in the world to have won four national awards, as well as a Chevy Bel Air convertible that ranked an amazing 990 out of 1,000 points at a national show.

Ever a perfectionist, Schmidt has been tasked with turning Patch's classic cars into concours-condition models. That work is oftentimes daunting. Patch once explained his economic strategy for collecting – and producing near-100-point cars:

"If you buy a car that is already an almost perfect 90 pointer, it takes you as much money to get those last

Top: Dodge's Custom Royal was that firm's flagship, featuring unique chrome tailfins, an upscale interior and the hemi 270 Super Red Ram engine. Bottom: "Fireball" Roberts joined the Ford factory team in 1956 and won five Grand National races that year alone. In 1957 he won eight races and finished 6th in the points championship.

Fantastic '57

Historians look upon 1957 in America as a time filled with prosperity and optimism. It was an electric year. The air was thick with the tunes of rock 'n roll and the buzz of new technology. The Russians launched Sputnik, inaugurating the Space Race, and federal troops forced integration at schools in Little Rock, Ark. On most of Americans' television sets were "Leave it to Beaver", "Gunsmoke", "Father Knows Best", and, of course, "American Bandstand". This was the year of Elvis (who had four songs on the Top 10), President Eisenhower (who began his second term in office), and Hank Aaron (who was the National League's MVP).

It was also the year of some of the country's most memorable automobiles.

Much was riding on the new American 1957 models. Lackluster sales in 1956 depressed the country's major manufacturers; U.S. output had dropped below '55 levels and at one point it was reported that 850,000 cars were overcrowding inventory lots. Output for the first half of 1956 was 1.3 million cars below same-period production of the previous year.

But sales were defibrillated as the year closed. The '57 models, credited by some as America's finest examples of styling, had made their debut.

Cars in the Chrysler Group caught the crowds' eye with its new styling direction. Lines were clean and low, with bodies that featured matte-finished aluminum grilles and high, sharp tail fins on new chassis. The white-and-gold De Soto Golden Adventurer, with its more powerful powerplant, drew plenty of gazes, as did the new Saratoga line. The magnificent Imperial shared the year's most powerful engine – a 6428cc V8 – with the big New Yorker. Chrysler also introduced its new Torque-flite transmission that combined a torque converter with a three-speed planetary gear set, controlled by push buttons.

General Motors was also championing fins, while adhering to chief stylist Harley Earl's mandate for lengthening and lowering bodies. Cadillac bore the most obvious of these traits, with height cut by up to 3 inches and center pillars removed from all models save the limousine. For all GM models, new engineering technology came in the form of the optional Powerglide torque converter. The Turboglide, an option for the most powerful engine, featured three turbines and two gear sets that were coupled to make gear changes imperceptible.

Chevrolet came out for '57 with 20 different models, including hardtops, sedans, convertibles, station wagons and a sports car (introduced in '53, the Corvette). Lines were lower on Chevy models, and, of course, tail fins were higher, and rolled aluminum panels could be added to the exterior of the popular Bel Air series. When all the color options were factored in, customers could essentially choose from 460 different vehicles.

Ford also came out with longer and lower bodies, 19 models in all. Of note were the Fairlane Custom and the Station Wagon series, as well as the Thunderbird sports car with a new grille, tail fins of its own, and a 5.1-liter engine with copper lead bearings and four-barrel carburetor that produced 245 bhp.

Struggling Studebaker Packard rolled out its line of Hawks, which were also lower, following the trend for sleeker styling. What would become one of automotive history's lessons of poor management, the company would face its demise soon, despite innovative designs and advanced engineering, as seen in its '57 offerings.

Towards the end of 1957, the threat of an oil crisis in the Middle East further distanced the prospect of owning larger, more powerful cars for many buyers. This was especially true for Europeans, who were facing fuel rationing.

10 points as it does to bring a much cheaper car up 80 points. A lot of choices depend not simply on the cool model but the condition it's in. If you can buy a 30–point car for $15,000 or a 90–point car for $70,000, it makes more sense to buy the cheaper one."

Schmidt's numerous connections have also proved invaluable in tracking down many of the rare gems in the collection.

"I love the fact that the display isn't just appealing to people who grew up when I did. Young kids just love the cars and appreciate them like they are works of art, which I believe they are. I might have expected the men who visit to love them, but I am gratified by the overwhelming reaction from women as well."
—Glenn Patch

"There are some other really neat cars from '57, but we just don't have any more room at this point," Schmidt said. "With what we have now, though, you could have gone to all the auto shows that year and not see every convertible made in 1957. There is no place on Earth before '57 Heaven – and I'll guarantee there will never be another – where you can see every American convertible made in '57. In addition there are hardtops, wagons and others. It's a unique collection for a person to focus in on just one year."

Another interesting and well-connected personality is Ralph Hurley, general manager of '57 Heaven. Hurley, who is retired from the U.S. Navy with 20 years service working in various areas including auto mechanics and body and paint work, was once employed as president of a large full-line Cessna Airplane dealership in Georgia. He later started Kansas Aircraft Corp. and Kansas City Aircraft Engines. For many years he ferried aircraft and helicopters all over the world for various aircraft dealers. Hurley met Patch roughly 30 years ago when he sold Patch an airplane. A close friendship ensued, as did sporadic working relationships.

Hurley has also been an owner and investor in several specialty auto sales companies, restaurants and lounges. Today he has a classic-car sales facility near the complex. It's no surprise that his continued love affair with

Pontiac's Bonneville was one of the GM models that featured fuel injection, a first for a few makes in 1957.

automobiles has at its heart 1957 models: his first new off-the-lot car was a 1957 Plymouth Fury.

According to Hurley, the collection welcomes 400-500 visitors per day, except on Mondays when no shows are scheduled. Even on Mondays Schmidt says 150-200 people will drop in to see the cars.

Promotions include television spots, print ads, announced specials and "everything that you can do to get customers," Hurley said. "We are also developing an outdoor area that will be called Area 57 that should attract even more crowds. There will be outdoor events, car shows, along with an old fifties-type drive-in theater."

It is Patch's intention to give visitors something more than just a touch of nostalgia, a quick feel-good takeaway. The goal is to send people home with an appreciation for what made the '50s great. Exactly what that is proves difficult to pin down.

"It's hard to say why the '50s appeal to so many people. Maybe it's because life was simpler then, or there are good memories associated with that time. But there's something more to it, because we see people of all ages coming in looking at the cars and watching the shows. There's a younger set of people, a new set of people, appreciating the same things that we enjoyed when we were young. It was a special time."

To learn more about '57 Heaven and Dick Clark's American Bandstand Theater Complex, call 1-877-LUV-1957 or visit www.AmericanBandstandTheater.com. AQ

Design for the 1957 De Soto Fire Flite design was bold and radical with tail fins, dual oval exhaust, and triple lens taillights. Chrysler Group cars built during 1957 sported spectacular design but were plagued with poor quality. Some of the models leaked and were unable to keep the rain out of the vehicle. Others had defective transmissions, power-steering units and a slew of other problems. These issues led to the downfall of De Soto and the eventual end of production.

For 1957, the 300-C (above) and the New Yorker were the most expensive and elaborate offerings in Chrysler showrooms. The 300-C literally defined all that was positive and progressive about the new Forward Look style that had the automotive press and buyers buzzing. Few cars before or since have so successfully packaged refined levels of performance, handling and styling as did the 300-C.

For 1957, Chevrolet produced 2,244 Cameo pickup trucks. The half-ton pickups were stylized with a panoramic windshield, hooded headlights and other special accents.

Squaring Motor Sport's Circle

Although the most private of persons, Max Mosley plays the most public of roles as president of the world federation of motoring clubs. Overcoming an inherited handicap, his colorful high-speed career has shown remarkable concentration, dedication and inspiration.

BY KARL LUDVIGSEN

Fahrenheit thermometers were in triple digits as cars clustered on the dummy grid at Kyalami for the South African Grand Prix on March 7, 1970. Strolling among them were two tall men in short-sleeved shirts, one dark-haired and 30 and the other reddish-blond and 29. They smiled broadly as they looked over the 23-car field of which their March 701s accounted for more than one-fifth. Though this was the first Formula 1 race for March, two of their cars were bang in the front row.

Said the blond, Max Mosley, we were "savoring the whole thing. Everything we'd set out to do, we'd done. There were two of our cars sitting at the front with equal times. You could feel the annoyance, hatred almost, of some of the Grand Prix establishment because we'd pulled it off. We'd only rented the building next to the dairy six months earlier. It was one of the most extraordinary moments of my life. It was an exhilarating time. Nothing seemed impossible."

To win the race would have been a miracle too far, but in the very next Grand Prix in Spain in April the winner was Jackie Stewart in a March. At the following race in Monaco March's Max Mosley and Colin Chapman of Lotus were discussing business

issues with Louis Stanley, major domo of the BRM team, when the pompous Stanley grew impatient with Mosley's eloquence.

"Dash it all, Mosley," he blustered, "you can't expect to come into Grand Prix racing and show us all how it's done in your first year!"

"Well," said a grinning Chapman, "he hasn't done badly so far!"

At the end of the 1970 season the Lotus chief admitted to March engineer Robin Herd that "the only reason I brought my team to America was to stop you bastards from winning the championship in your first year!" As it was March finished a strong third in the world manufacturers' championship just behind Lotus and Ferrari.

Few racing-car builders stepped on to the world stage with the panache, mystery and sensation of March. This was the handiwork of young Mosley, whose task it was as the company's head of finance and sponsorship to weave a convincing web of cred-

ibility for a complete newcomer to racing that aimed to compete all the way up to Formula 1. He did this so compellingly that many were persuaded that cubic Deutchmarks were flowing in from German conglomerates thought to be March's "mystery backers."

After "the building next to the dairy" was occupied Mosley revealed March's existence on Oct. 1, 1969, and its Formula 1 aims a month later. The racing world was on tenterhooks until Feb. 10, 1970, when it was sum-

Above left: Max Mosley in 1969 during the preparations for the launch of March Engineering. Above: Mosely is being followed by the similar Brabham of Xavier Perrot, who finished 10th to Max's 8th at Monza, June 23, 1968.

moned to a cold, sunny Silverstone to see what March had wrought. With engineer Robin Herd, car-builder Graham Coaker and team manager Alan Rees, Max Mosley was center-stage as Grand Prix cars were rolled out for Chris Amon, Mario Andretti and – something of a coup – reigning world champion Jackie Stewart. On that blustery day March shrugged off its nickname of Much-Advertised Racing-Car Hoax.

In fact March Engineering Ltd. was founded on a scant £2,500 from each of its four partners. "I felt that

Mosely with his Brabham BT23C at Monza for the Formula 2 race on June 23, 1968. His 8th-place finish of 22 starters was helped by seven of the leading racers crashing out on lap 22 of 45.

if you had enough talent and you assembled the right people," said Mosley, "the money would simply come in. We thought that if we put it all together, announced it all and made a big enough thing out of it, the sponsors would pour in, the suppliers wouldn't ask for payment particularly promptly and the thing would get off the ground." Though it wasn't quite that easy, that's exactly what happened – helped by cubic Deutchmarks from Porsche to provide a Formula 1 seat for its star driver Jo Siffert.

Thus was launched on the world stage the motor-racing career of Max Rufus Mosley. In 1970, in which he would turn 30 in April, he was described by Ted Simon as "a tallish, slight figure in a striped shirt and fawn corduroys. He was so thin that between his bones and his closely cut clothing there seemed hardly to be room for any flesh at all. The face was pale, the cheekbones prominent, the hair a dusty red color which also arched bushily over large cold gray eyes. It was

a young face, unnaturally knowing, which one might have found on a subaltern in the First World War."

Addressing colleagues, said Simon, Mosley "stooped from the hips, his hands fluttering in a gesture of conciliation. He seemed to be emphasizing his physical fragility, but it should not be mistaken for weakness. When he chose he could pull himself up so taut that he cut the atmosphere around him like a knife."

These characteristics are not unfamiliar to the many who have since known Max Mosley during his climb to the top of the tree of world motoring as the president of the international federation of motoring clubs, the Paris-based Federation Internationale de l'Automobile or FIA. Abstemiousness and sports, first skiing and then snowboarding, have kept his lanky frame slender. The cheeks are broader and the hair graying but the eyes still penetrate. Mosley is the quintessence of politeness, sometimes taken to politesse, in his personal contacts. Yet those who assume that his aristocratic civility

implies lack of resolve are doomed to disappointment.

Some are concerned that the dichotomy may be intensifying between Mosley's public tact and the rigorous policies he implements on behalf of the FIA. "I was in a meeting with him the other day," said a senior Formula 1 engineer, "in which he was the essence of reasonableness and calm. Yet afterward he wrote the most scathing possible letter to all the participants." Mosley is good at seeming to listen. Indeed he invites comment from all parties. But this doesn't imply that the resulting rules and rulings will necessarily take those views into account.

This is important, because Mosley's FIA has disseminated its intentions for dramatic changes in the Formula 1 cars of the future. High points are as follows:

2008:

Possible restrictions on the use of wind tunnels and removal of aerodynamic appendages on cars, subject to agreement by the teams.

2009:

Cutting aerodynamic downforce in half by means not yet specified.

Fitting cars with devices that will recover braking energy and allow drivers to use the recovered energy for a specified time during each lap.

2010:

Recovery of both waste heat and exhaust energy and its use to propel the car.

Addressing aerodynamics either by creating standard designs or by introducing road-car elements or both.

2011:

Replacement of present 2.4-liter V8 engine by a new design using biofuels, turbocharged and restricted in output by the use of limits on the maximum flow of fuel energy to the engine.

Replacement of emphasis on aerodynamics by a new freedom of chassis and suspension design, using electronics to make the car more energy-efficient.

Anyone reading this list of high-tech revisions to the world's leading racing formula who felt that their provisions would be over the head of the FIA's chief would be in grievous error. Having gained a degree in physics at Oxford's Christchurch College, Mosley is capable of his own computations and conclusions on technical matters.

"You can brief him on the most intricate technical matters and he gets it first time," said Peter Wright, a motor-racing engineer and advisor to the FIA. "He understands the fundamental principles behind the engineering. He even comes back with his own interpretation. Then he goes off and does his politics with the full knowledge of what he's talking about. You underestimate him at your peril."

"Though we didn't know each other at the time," added Robin Herd, the dark-haired engineer who walked the Kyalami pit lane with Mosley, "we read physics together at Oxford. Max is a pretty competent technical guy. He's sort of a technical director, not a designer. At March he would work with one of the drivers and I'd do the other, engineering the cars to the circuits."

On one occasion during March's baptismal 1970 season Mosley gave a different kind of advice to his lead driver, Chris Amon. "The 701 was a very basic car and the only way you could make it go was to drive it on the throttle and slide it around a bit," said Chris. In one qualifying session he was doing just that, "coming round the corner on to the pit straight with the tail out in total oversteer. When I came in to the pits, Max bent down into the cockpit and said, 'Would you mind coming through that corner a little differently? It's making the car look bad.'"

During his tenure at the FIA Mosley has used his knowledge of both physics and politics to force through substantial changes in the Formula 1 rules. "Over the years he's learned," said Herd, "that the greater the opposition to what he's proposed, the greater his certainty that he's correct, that he's got a sure-fire winner." Although Formula 1's rules are rigorously defined by the confidential Concorde Agreement, the FIA has the right to require changes for safety reasons, a loophole that Mosley has brilliantly exploited.

The introduction of grooved tires in the 1998 season

to reduce cornering power was a good example. "I had nothing to do at one of the Formula 1 meetings," Mosley recalled, "and I started to do calculations, very elementary ones, showing mathematically that if a car lost control on a corner it would spin for a distance exactly equal to half the radius of the corner. This is not magic, a really good schoolboy could do it. What came out of this was that you need to reduce the grip of the tires. The less the grip, the safer the car. And the lower the speed of the accident.

"Then I said to the tire companies that we now need to change what they call a 'land-sea' ratio, the proportion of rubber to the width of the tires. One of the tire company bosses said to me, 'If you're going to do that, keep it simple. Instead of having a tread pattern, just put a groove in it.' So that's where that idea came from. The concept that reduces the rubber on the road, that was mine. It was simple to have the grooves so everybody could understand them.

"That really did keep the speeds under control," Mosley added. "We are always told, 'Reduce the aerodynamics'" — the wings and underbody suc-

Mosley, age 25, with a group of fellow Clubman's racers in 1965. Mosley is the tall fellow on the right side with Esso driving suit.

Left: Max (in white coat) with Bernie Ecclestone in the pits at Monaco in 1980. Right: Crew chief Vincent Granatelli, at left, meets with March Engineering directors as STP-March Grand Prix cars are completed at the factory near Oxford, England. From left: Granatelli, Mosley, team manager Alan Rees, Graham Coaker and chief designer Robin Herd seated on wheel.

tion generation that create powerful grip – generating downforce. "Every time we tried to do something to the aerodynamics they'd catch it back up again. We have to make sure that the cars don't keep getting faster and faster with some very competent people trying to make sure they do go faster and faster. For 30 years we've been constantly trying to reduce the aerodynamic potential of the cars to keep the speeds in check and this has failed.

"So if you have a responsible governing body," continued Mosley, "you must have a final point of defense and that for us is the grooved tires. The only way that you really make a difference is by interfering with the fundamental parameters. The amount of rubber on the road is one and the engine capacity is another." With the deployment of similar logic the FIA succeeded in reducing engine size from 3.0-liter V10s to 2.4-liter V8s in 2006. "They're already talking about 750 to 800 horsepower," said Mosley, "but of course they'd have been way over 1,000 if we hadn't done it."

Though these changes have been substantial, those listed earlier for the years ahead are even more dramatic. This imposing and ambitious menu of advances has been propounded by a man who has declared his intention to step down as FIA president when his term ends in October 2009. Speculation over whether he'll actually do so is rife. In 2003 Mosley said, "My term of office ends in 2005. One should never stay too long and I am very sensitive to that." At the beginning of July 2004 he said he would resign early, in three months, but just over two weeks later he changed his mind.

"I'll probably get to 2009," Mosley said most recently, "but I think it would be absolutely wrong to be around for too long. There's a great danger that you start thinking you're indispensable." In fact, it is not easy for Mosley to envision an FIA run by someone of similar caliber – for people of such broad and deep knowledge and skill are not thick on the ground.

Magazine editor Matt Bishop remarked that "Mosley has positioned the FIA so that it straddles the worlds of politics and industry in a way that gives it great power

Mosley (left) talks shop with Rees (middle) and Herd around a Ford-Cosworth engine.

in the automotive world. Occupying the middle ground as it does, it is able to exert enormous influence in each area while never quite falling out with either camp." While the FIA has always commanded respect, representing as it does the more than 100 million members of 213 of the world's motoring clubs in 125 countries, it has indeed gained enhanced authority under Max Mosley's firm guidance.

With the FIA as his platform, Mosley has extended his influence to other organizations. He served a five-year term as the Honorary President of the European Parliament's Automobile Users Intergroup and was named to the board of the European Commission's CARS 21 Group at its formation in 2005 to promote global competitiveness for the European auto industry. Mosley's initiative was the creation of EuroNCAP, a cooperative program of crash testing that's now the yardstick for the impact-safety performance of all cars sold in Europe.

"EuroNCAP started in 1996," Max explained, "and it was entirely initiated by us. David Ward, the head of our Brussels office, was a key person there. The FIA financed it in the early days, almost entirely. We were putting in a million Euros a year at one stage and that got it going. Then certain cars were paid for by the British government, a little bit by the Swedish government. I resigned from it in 2004 simply because I hadn't time to go on doing it."

Operating as he does at a very high level, both nationally and internationally, it would be easy to envision a conventional political career for Max Mosley. In fact he did make a significant effort in the early 1980s to be accepted as a candidate for Britain's Parliament. Former prime minister "Harold Macmillan helped him a lot," said Herd, "and they tried very hard to get him accepted. But there was no way.

"He tried – and he was trying very hard – to get into the European Parliament in the 2005 lot," added Herd, "and not do a third stint as president of the FIA. The Blair government were thinking he would make a very good member of the European Parliament. But the same thing happened." In these negotiations conflicts arose with others in Britain's Labour government who envi-

Racing partners: Rees, Herd and Mosley over engineering detail drawings for the 1971 STP-March Grand Prix cars. March Engineering teamed with STP for the '71 season. Mosley was the firm's financial manager.

advocated peace negotiations with Germany after war broke out in September 1939. Under controversial Defence Regulation 18B he was arrested as a security risk on May 23, 1940, and imprisoned. On June 29, the police knocked on Diana's door. She was breastfeeding their second son, Max, who'd been born on April 13. She wasn't allowed to take him with her to Holloway Prison.

At 11 weeks, Max's nanny reported to Diana that "he is bonny and such a lovely color and sleeps so well and is just a sweet pet, always a happy smile." In 1943 Max and his older brother Alexander were allowed a two-night stay with the Mosleys at Holloway. "Weedoms" was the senior Mosley's nickname for Max. He also called him the "Entschlossener", which can be translated as resolute, determined or decisive. This was an insightful assessment of Max Mosley at age 3.

In November 1943 the Mosleys were released from Holloway. Still under house arrest, they moved to a house near Newbury where Diana assumed the role of educator to her sons. Neighborhood youngsters, she said, "taught them every swear word in the calendar." On their release at war's end the Mosleys bought Crowood Farm in Wiltshire. There Max became a fan of the football club of nearby Swindon and helped out with chores on the farm.

At Crowood Max enjoyed riding his pony, Johnny. This grew into an enthusiasm for the hunt when the family moved out of Britain in 1950. They acquired a house in Paris and a former bishop's palace in Ireland's County Galway. There Johnny's hoofbeats continued to be heard with Max riding to the hunt on every opportunity. "It was a paradise for sport," Diana Mosley recalled, "because the people are young in heart, quite without fear and always ready for a lark." This rubbed off on her youngest son.

"When my father moved out of England he took all his resources with him," Mosley recalled. "He lived abroad and died domiciled abroad, which had all sorts of advantages. He'd never had to work and my mother never had to work. The Mosley family owned a huge proportion of the land that the city of Manchester was built on. My father sold all the head leases, fortunately

sioned a future for Mosley in the House of Lords. This option too was foreclosed, at least for the time being.

What malignant force barred Mosley from mainstream British politics? It was, simply enough, his name. Max was the youngest son of a man who was nominated by a history professor in 2005 as the Worst Briton of the 20th Century. Born in 1896, inheritor of a baronetcy that dated from 1720, Oswald Mosley became the youngest Member of Parliament to take his seat in 1918. At first a Conservative, he later sided with Labour, under whose flag he served in the House of Commons to 1931.

A compelling personality of deep intellect with a magnetic appeal to women, Oswald Mosley was a dynamic orator and a man impatient with the sluggish pace of Britain between the wars. Having studied the

achievements of Mussolini in Italy, Mosley founded the British Union of Fascists in 1932. Offering a platform of anti-Communism and trade protectionism, the BUF attracted initial support from leading British dailies, claiming membership of 50,000. But its trappings of black shirts and lightning-strike banners began to repel more than they attracted.

After the death of his first wife Oswald Mosley married the ravishingly beautiful Diana Guinness, nee Mitford. The wedding took place in secret in the Berlin residence of Nazi propagandist Josef Goebbels, with Adolf Hitler among the guests, in 1936. Violence at some of its events, culminating that same year in a brawl in East London, brought discredit to Mosley and his British Fascists.

Oswald Mosley was among many in Britain who

before the war, to one of the big insurance companies. He sold other estates in Staffordshire, liquidating the family money and moving it out of England in 1950. So I go and talk to some rather elderly gentlemen when I need money." The FIA presidency is, of course, unpaid.

Had his much-reviled father let sleeping dogs lie after the war, or indeed been seen to manifest some repentance, Max might have been able to enjoy a career in politics. But this was not Sir Oswald's character. He returned to the hustings to promote the idea of a politically unified Europe, even starting a monthly magazine to campaign to that end, edited by the faithful Diana. His last general elections were fought in 1959 and 1966, without success. Oswald Mosley died in France in December 1980.

Private tutoring ended for Max at age 13 when he was sent off to Schule Schloss Stein at Stein an der Traun in Germany's Bavaria. Foreshadowing the young man's future was the ownership of the Schloss or castle and its brewery in the early 20th century by the noble Arco-Zinneberg family. Fraternal Counts Max and Engelbert Arco-Zinneberg were active motor-racers from 1929 to 1932 driving Mercedes-Benz, Austro-Daimler and Amilcar machinery.

Mosley left Bavaria after 18 months with a good command of German to go with his already fluent French. "When I came back to England at 15 I had a bit of catching up to do," he recalled, "but I did catch up. I went to school in England for a year." This could be the period of which he remarked, "I got expelled from one school following a slight misunderstanding with a teacher who found me in the girls' dormitory.

"When I was 16 my parents let me go and live in London on my own – which was very nice. I was in Bloomsbury the first year and the second year in Holland Park Avenue. I went to Soho every single night for the first year because I was near Soho. I used to go to all the places where rock 'n roll was starting. And then when I was 18 I went to Oxford.

"At Oxford I was the first person in Christchurch to wear jeans," said Max. "In those days the vast majority had done their National Service and they'd turn up in a jacket and tie and a pair of trousers. I was in jeans like people are nowadays. Once the porter came after me and said, 'Are you a member of this college, sir?'"

Mosley elected to study physics because it offered "the certainty of science and also the precision of it all. I liked the idea that in a sense you didn't have to discuss things, like politicians do. I think that was because of the example of my father. You make the thing and you conduct the experiment and it works or it doesn't work. But it became quite obvious that I didn't have the capacities to be the person to make the big discovery. So when I'd done the three years and got a degree I stopped."

In his last year at Oxford Mosley showed why he'd been nicknamed the "Entschlossener": "Somebody said to me, 'There's no way you could ever compete in the Oxford Union Debating Society.' Scientists didn't do that. So of course the next day I was down there! I became secretary of the Union, which was unheard-of for somebody from the science side. Also I had this political background because of my father, which wasn't exactly a help. By that time I realized that what I really ought to do was something like the law, so the minute I left Oxford I started reading for the bar."

In fact his Oxford Union ambitions didn't prevent the loyal 22-year-old Mosley from assisting his father in his political campaigns. When some toughs attacked Sir Oswald in East London in 1962 Max came to his aid, only to be bundled into a van by the police along with the assailants. At a hearing the next morning he stated that it wasn't for him to stand idly by while his father was beaten, that "it was not only my right but my duty to go to his aid."

Max was already a married man, having met Jean Taylor, a year younger. They tied the knot in July 1960. "I'd known her for about three years," Mosley recalled. "She was the one who was working. The person she worked for used to be a racing marshal in his spare time. He had a couple of tickets for a race at Silverstone and couldn't go. He said, 'Would you like to go with your husband?' and so we went. It was the Daily Express Trophy in 1961. And it was won by Stirling Moss who in the wet lapped the entire field.

"There was the usual traffic jam so we were a little

Mosley with Chris Amon at the March launch in February 1970.

Herd stood to address the press at the March launch in February 1970. Mosley was two places to his left and on the right were Granatelli and Mario Andretti.

bit late," Max continued. "They'd started the Formula Junior race and I'd just got to the barrier at Woodcote in time to see them come over the hill under the Daily Express bridge – and I was just transfixed. I'd never seen anything like it. It was an instant addiction."

Not yet having access to the Mosley millions, Max had to find a way to scratch this new itch. "After I graduated I went to a racing drivers school at Finmere, which was just down the road from Silverstone. It was an aerodrome with a very primitive track, just for this drivers school. I used to do a few laps in a really rubbishy old car. It cost a pound a lap, more than I could afford, but I did it. It was enough to make me realize that I was hooked."

Not having studied law at university, Mosley had to start from scratch on his legal career. "That was okay," he said, masking the considerable effort required. "By the time I was 24 I was called to the bar. Then I started teaching law in the evenings. Though I hadn't done the degree myself, I used to teach people at London University. You'd be half a page ahead of them in the textbook, just beginning to understand it yourself, and explaining it to them – anyway they all seemed happy.

"We used to get paid quite well for that," Max added. "By teaching law in evening classes I was able to accumulate enough money to get a Clubman's racing car. And by teaching through the winter I could then pay for the racing in the summer." A starting point for many in the sport, the Clubman's car was a shrewdly simple machine with a Ford four-cylinder engine of 1.0 or 1.5 liters depending on class. Although many racers built their own, most popular was Arthur Mallock's serviceable U2, one of which Mosley acquired for 1966.

"The first race I went to was at Snetterton. I'd no idea of what would happen. I just turned up for the race. I didn't even know how to start it. I had to get it off the trailer by myself; nobody was with me. The only way I could think to get it started was to take it down the scrutineering bay and see if the scrutineers would start it for me. And then in the race – because everybody left and I was sitting there – somebody gave me a push start so I set off on my own behind them.

"I was driving around Snetterton thinking, 'I can't do any good here. I'll never catch the leaders, but for sure I'll have fastest lap because it felt really fast.' And then the leaders came past me and I realized that they were flat out where I was braking. I think I was something like 20 seconds off the pace. So that gave me a little inkling of what it was all about. Before long I was

keeping up with them."

Mosley made another important discovery. "In one of my first races they put the practice times up, a list of people and their times as they do. All the competitors in that class of racing were looking at the list and they came to my name. I heard somebody say, 'Mosley, Max Mosley. He must be some relation of Alf Mosley, the coachbuilder.' I thought to myself, 'I've found a world where they don't know about Oswald Mosley.' And it has been a bit like that in motor racing: nobody gives a darn."

Heartened by these discoveries, now earning more as a practicing barrister, Mosley prepared well for 1967. In the tiny premises of Meedspeed in Walthamstow he helped Dave Reeves build up his U2 over the winter, turning his hand to machining and fabrication. "The very first race the following year was at Snetterton and this time I won; only just, but I did. We had a really good season in '67." This was indeed so. Mosley took part in 22 Clubman's events and won 10 times, setting fastest lap on eight occasions.

"Arthur Mallock, who made the U2s, sometimes used to race in Formula 2 by taking the mudguards off," Mosely said. "There was an unanswerable argument that it was a single-seater. So I turned up at Crystal Palace for a Formula 2 race in '67 with this thing. The scrutineer said, 'You can't bring that thing in here!' Of course with a barrister background I explained that I could. Anyway, they accepted it. I found myself in the collecting area and there were Bruce McLaren and John Surtees and Jacky Ickx and everybody and me in my old U2.

"That race was another huge eye-opener because there's a very fast corner at the top, one of those corners that tightens on you, the main corner at the end of the straight. Going out on the track with these people, I realized that they were putting the brakes on where I was taking them off. Armed with the knowledge I picked up there I put the mudguards back on and went to Brands Hatch. On the short circuit at Brands, the so-called Indy Circuit, I took 1.6 seconds off the lap record, which was a lot – all learned from watching the hot shoes."

Hobnobbing at Crystal Palace on May 29, 1967, with the royalty of motor racing was a heady experience for the 27-year-old Mosley. The Formula 2 for 1.6-liter production-based engines was taken up enthusiastically by British builders Brabham, Chevron, Lotus and McLaren while France's Matra and Italy's Tecno were also contenders. Most used the Ford-based Cosworth FVA 16-valve four.

To move up to Formula 2 Max invested in one of the quick combinations, an FVA-powered Brabham BT23C, for 1968. He bought it from Frank Williams, who was graduating from driving to team ownership and management. For economies of scale Mosley teamed up with Chris Lambert, already a Formula 2 racer, to form the London Racing Team. This only lasted through the first few races of 1968, however:

"I can't remember what happened with the London Racing Team but it didn't work. I think my mechanic, John Redgrave, suggested moving the car to Frank Williams. I had all these dealings with Frank anyway so we went down there." From mid-June Williams was the entrant, with Mosley driving his car when Williams's lead driver, Piers Courage, was busy with Formula 1. Tragically Mosley's original partner, Lambert, was killed in a crash at Zandvoort at the end of July. Max himself crashed out later in the same race, but without injury.

"Chris's father pursued it for years," said Mosley, in "a long battle to find out what happened. It took a lot of the fun out of it for me." It was in fact a sobering season. Mosley's first race at Hockenheim on April 7 was the one in which Jim Clark was killed. Early in July popular French driver Jo Schlesser died in a flaming crash at Rouen. This was a harsh exposure to the hazards of racing.

"You just wanted to do it so much that you were prepared to take the risk," Max admitted. "I was a very rational person, age 28, who realized that there were just two very thin aluminum petrol tanks, held by tie wraps in a steel-tube frame, with a little bit of fiberglass round the outside, in which we were reaching speeds of 170 mph at places like Hockenheim.

"If you said anything to anybody in those days they

In the McLaren race garage: Mosley, facing the camera, meets with Dr. Sid Watkins, uniformed, and McLaren team principal Ron Dennis.

always had two arguments," Mosley added. "They said you don't have to do it if you don't want to – perfectly true. And if you think the corner is dangerous you should slow down a bit. Of course it's nonsense to say, 'Slow down.' If you presented one of today's Grand Prix drivers with two cars and said, 'That one's very, very safe; this one is extremely dangerous but the dangerous one is two seconds a lap quicker,' they'll pick the dangerous one."

This higher level of the sport challenged Mosley. However "the resolute one" was not about to admit defeat. He was rightly pleased with an eighth-place finish on June 23 at Monza, where a dozen entrants failed to qualify. After Lambert's death he only returned to the wars at Vallelunga near Rome at the end of October, placing 14th on the aggregate of two heats.

What did the established stars make of this patrician interloper? "Max was the oddball," recalled Jackie Oliver, "for why he was there and the way he used to dress. We used to take the piss out of him most of the time. He was an intellectual, so that was quite unusual for racers then. And he used to wear an awful long fur coat, even when it wasn't cold. I think he was trying to make some sort of statement. I suppose that wasn't unusual for the 1960s."

"I wasn't sure what I was going to do in 1969," Mosley said, "so I did a deal with Len Street to race a Lotus 59B-Cosworth." He ventured all the way to Jarama in Spain for a Formula Libre race on April 13 in which only eight cars started. Although classified as a retirement with injector problems, Mosley reckoned he was seventh. It was a tribute to his expository skills that he was able to fill two pages of Autosport with a detailed and enthralling account of one of racing's less significant events.

Not only as a journalist but also as a barrister Mosley's career was flourishing. To take advantage of his physics he elected to specialize in patent law. This had another advantage, he admitted: "The Patent and Trademark Chambers gave you the freedom to do things like go racing. You could say to your clerk, 'I can't be here on Friday because I'm at Monza.' You couldn't do that at the criminal bar or really even the common-law bar. Because if you were on at the Old Bailey, you couldn't just move it."

In one major case Mosley was part of the team that acted for Bayer of Germany to regain control of its cross-shaped logo, world-famous on packs of Bayer aspirin, denied them by victors in two world wars. "Our case was that a custodian of enemy property can take what he likes but when people see that cross they think of Bayer Leverkusen. From Bayer's point of view we got a very acceptable settlement. They paid a certain amount of money and got it back. I like to think they paid a lot less money than they would have paid otherwise."

Mosley also spent the early 1960s jumping out of airplanes: "I did 22 jumps, some of them on exercises with all the gear and equipment." This was as a mem-

ber of the Parachute Regiment of Britain's Territorial Army, the equivalent of America's National Guard. "I always felt that you ought to have some sort of military experience, so if you're going to do it you may as well join, if you can, one of the elite regiments. I spent three years doing that. We didn't see any action or anything, just exercises.

"After 1965 I got busy and I had to stop," Mosley recalled. "But it taught me a lot of things. It taught me how much longer you can go on when you think you're too tired to continue. It also taught me that if you're walking along and you start to feel tired the trick is to walk a bit faster. Yes, if your legs start to feel tired you walk faster." The Entschlossener was invigorated, not daunted, by the demands of the military.

The Eifelrennen at the daunting Nürburgring on April 27, 1969, was a valedictory racing appearance for Mosley. Still more than a minute and a half from the pole time in practice for his Formula 2 race, he crashed when the suspension of his Lotus disassembled itself. "I decided to stop after that. I realized I wasn't going to be world champion. By then I had gotten to know a lot of people who were, or would

go on to become, important parts of motor racing."

One of them was Robin Herd. "We slightly knew each other at Oxford but we weren't friends, really," Mosley said. "He was much more of a sportsman than me. He represented his college in I don't know how many sports. He was a big cricket player, very good at water polo and tennis and soccer and all those sorts of ball games." During Mosley's 1968 racing season they met again at the Williams workshop on Bath Road: "I was at Frank's lock-up one evening when in walked Robin, who was moonlighting from McLaren by modifying the rear suspension on Piers's car.

"We went off and had dinner somewhere and immediately realized that we both felt something should be done, that the racing world needed a bit of a shakeup. We thought alike, had very similar sorts of approaches. Also it was obvious, quite apart from his academic record, that Robin was very, very clever. You don't meet many clever people in motor racing. We both felt that we could do better than the existing people."

Thus the seeds of March were planted. They began to fructify in April 1969, when the first serious discussions were held. Sir Oswald told his son, "You'll almost certainly go bust, but it will be good training

for something serious later on." March survived well into the 1970s as a car builder but its Formula 1 fortunes deteriorated to an ignominious ninth in the constructors' championship in 1974, recovering to seventh in 1976 before ceasing Grand Prix participation.

March's first year in Formula 1, 1970, also found Max and Jean Mosley starting a family: "My eldest son, Alexander, came along in April 1970. Then the second son, Patrick, came in February of 1972. We became country-based in 1970 and then in '71 we acquired a small cottage near Bicester, which we still have." While Mosley is now Monaco-based for tax reasons, Jean lives in London. The family meets up at a house in France's Var district.

In 1977 Max Mosley officially withdrew from March. "He'd had enough of running an engineering company," Herd remembered. "In a very honorable way he made sure that we had sponsorship of our programs for 1978. Max spoiled me, because I thought all commercial directors were like this, totally trustworthy. He's one of those lovely people who takes what he does seriously but doesn't take himself seriously. He created the foundation of what we were able to do at Indy."

"I sold my shares to Robin," Mosley said. "And as

soon as I got out of course March started making sensible money! He had his great success with Indy cars; I think one year 31 out of the 33 cars running were theirs." "Max never really left March," Herd added. "He always kept in touch. We had lengthy beery talks over the Formula 1 engine question. In 1988 Max and I were the first to see BMW's V10 engine for Formula 1."

By 1978 Mosley was increasingly involved with the legal and commercial affairs of the Formula One Constructors Association, FOCA, formed by entrepreneur and Brabham team owner Bernie Ecclestone. The latter, another of those rare clever people in motor racing, stepped into a vacuum left by race organizers who were unaware of the potential of television and team owners who preferred to leave the negotiations to someone else. He spotted the talent of Mosley, who from 1971 was FOCA's legal advisor.

Bound by mutual respect, the two men dared to clash with the head of the FIA over racing's commercial and operational jurisdiction. Ecclestone's biographer, Terry Lovell, wrote that Mosley "has been the political strategist throughout much of the commercial and political development of Formula 1, while Ecclestone has been the enforcer with the razor-sharp negotiating brain. Neither could have achieved his level of power, influence and wealth without the close alliance of the other."

In the early 1980s Mosley stepped out of FOCA because "if I don't get out of this I'll be doing this when I'm 60. I did a few other bits and pieces here and there. I did a couple of things with Bernie, nothing to do with motor racing. And then it seemed to me that I'd got such a big capital invested in the sense of what I knew about the sport I thought I'd make a comeback. I came back as chairman of the Manufacturers Commission, representing the world motor industry on the FIA's World Council. That was in 1986."

Mosley was parachuted into the chairmanship of this commission by Jean-Marie Balestre, the blustery but powerful Frenchman who had long dominated the affairs of the FIA and its sporting arm, FISA. During Mosley's FOCA years the two had frequently crossed swords over the issue of commercial rights

to Formula 1 racing. Mosley and Ecclestone went so far as to formulate a "World Federation of Motor Sports" to administer "The World Professional Drivers Championship" independently of the FIA. "That was the winter of 1980-81, Mosley recalled, "because then we signed the Concorde agreement at the beginning of March 1981. The Concorde agreement came out of that." Both were drafted by Mosley.

Mosley's tenure as chairman of the FIA's Manufacturers Commission, rewarded by a handsome stipend that Balestre had wangled from the car manufacturers, "worked very well for some years but toward the end of 1990 I became completely frustrated because I could never get Balestre on the phone to talk about problems. I had various decisions to make and I couldn't get an answer. I thought, this is so tiresome I'm going to stop. I was fed up with it."

Mosley then decided – "I'd nothing to lose" – to run against Balestre for the presidency of the FISA. Although the incumbent had a formidable political machine, oiled by the favors he was able to grant to national clubs in the form of positions and events, Mosley shrewdly campaigned in the remoter regions that felt alienated from the controversial Balestre. In 1991 he succeeded in toppling Jean-Marie from his FISA post.

Balestre remained in charge of the FIA. This too was destined to change in 1993, when the FISA and FIA merged and Mosley was elected to head the global organization. He faced his first sporting crisis in 1994, when Roland Ratzenberger and the great Ayrton Senna were killed in their Formula 1 cars at Imola. Responding to that terrible weekend, said FIA medical advisor Dr. Sid Watkins, "he's revolutionized safety. He's supported every initiative without question and provided the money to finance it, which has been

Mosley, on the phone, confers with a colleague at the FIA's Paris offices.

enormously expensive."

Not all Mosley's initiatives have been crowned with success. An attempt to introduce 3.5-liter engines in international sports-car racing in 1991 was a failure. More recently he championed the cause of the independent teams in Formula 1, only to see the sole independent engine supplier, Cosworth, be pushed out of the sport.

Teams backed and supplied by car manufacturers now dominate Formula 1, although Mosley has always maintained that car makers are too fickle to be relied upon as partners at racing's top level. This was one of his main arguments in the FIA's successful campaign to keep the auto makers from establishing a separate Grand Prix series, a struggle, he says, which was "about who wields political power over the commercial side of Formula 1 and who gets what money.".

At a Formula 1 race in Japan, Mosley shakes hands with Jean Todt, a team principal of Ferrari.

In some phases of his FIA career Mosley has been reviled by the Formula 1 teams for his seemingly arbitrary rulemaking. One example was his unwillingness to allow a chicane to be built to allow Grand Prix racing to continue with all the teams at Indianapolis in 2005 after Michelin admitted that its tires weren't up to the job. But ultimately the team principals have come to respect him for the clarity of his thinking and expression.

"Max has been doing an extremely good job," said Jean Todt of Ferrari. "He's committed – sometimes a bit too committed. He follows the sport closely. He's well informed. Whenever you call him, he returns your call. He's consistent. He goes to his office every day. We in Formula 1 are unable to agree on any kind of evolution, so in the end he has to decide these things. Sometimes it is good; sometimes it is not good. But it's very much by respect for his policy that often we have to encourage him to move forward, even if I feel that it's not the best for Ferrari."

If all the teams are united in their opposition to his proposals, Mosley is happy. "We've tried to understand the problems," he told Peter Windsor, "and then to make an independent decision that doesn't take into account any of the vested interests of the teams. They don't like it, but then why should they? We, the FIA, do not exist in order to help one party or another. The opposite, indeed, is true."

A consummately self-contained individual, Mosley is not what the British call "clubbable." He's not a target of the paparazzi in society hangouts or the hot spots along the Grand Prix trail. "I'm not very sociable, I suppose," he once remarked. "He's rather shy and reserved," said Dr. Sid Watkins. "He's rather nervous when he has to speak publicly. He manages the FIA's World Council in a remarkable manner. He's at his best when he's on his feet, a typical barrister."

Never happier than when catching an adversary out and scheming to one-up him, Mosley takes personal pleasure from his challenging days in the office. When especially delighted he'll manifest what's called "the Mosley laugh: a quiet chuckle accompanied by a creasing-up of the face as if some much larger eruption of mirth is imminent."

Creasing of the presidential cheeks occurred when Mosley laughingly mentioned some ideas that he has in reserve to slow down the Formula 1 cars: "I've two things left in my armory which I've never told anybody about. One is speed bumps in the pit lane – because the rules don't say I can't do this. The other one is the FIA's randomly controlled sprinklers, water sprinklers around the course. So you have to use completely different tires to cope with this." Laugh if you will, but Mosley is not lacking in creativity.

Mosley's achievements have been recognized by his peers in his reelections to the leadership of the FIA. Among his honors are Germany's Golden VdM Dieselring, Italy's Order of Merit, France's Légion d'Honneur and in Britain the Gold Medal of the Institute of the Motor Industry. In 2005 he was the recipient of an honorary Doctorate of Civil Law from Northumbria University.

What could the future hold for this multi-talented man? "Politics on a broader scale would be interesting," he admits, while acknowledging the constraints he inherited from his father. "Equally, I would like nothing more than to spend a year or two traveling from one classical music festival to another and, between venues, having time to read, to think and to reflect." Might this remarkable individual ever have that opportunity? Not so long as the world of motoring feels it needs Max Mosley in charge.

Beauties of Switzerland

Carrosserie Gebrüder Beutler & Co., Thun

I n the years after World War II, Swiss customers with sophisticated taste who were looking for something special still had the luxury of coachbuilt bodies fitted by Graber, Worblaufen, Tüscher and Gebrüder Beutler of Thun. The creations of Beutler excelled by a singular, elegant design and top-quality workmanship.

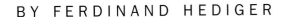

BY FERDINAND HEDIGER

Ernst (born 1915) and Fritz (born 1914) Beutler had a solid professional background. Both had served their apprenticeship and worked in various renowned Swiss coachbuilding companies. Most influential was their job with Carrosserie Worblaufen (see *Automobile Quarterly*, Vol. 39 No. 4), where they both worked from 1937 to 1942. While Fritz was masterly handling the special machine that shaped sheet-metal, Ernst showed a remarkable talent for creating new designs. During the war both served in the Swiss Army. Due to the lack of gasoline there was no demand for special-bodied passenger cars. According to his own words, Ernst began to work on his own in 1943. In the beginning this consisted mainly in fitting wood-gas generators to passenger cars as a substitute to gasoline.

Despite the difficult conditions the Beutler brothers founded their own coachbuilding company in 1946 and had a new workshop built in Thun. The first car to obtain a Beutler cabriolet was on a French Salmson chassis. In 1947-48 a Healey with a distinguished, ele-

The marques that utilized Beutler were as prestigious as they were varied. Seen here: A 1947 Healey 2.4 liter coupé (top and left) and the 1948 Porsche 356 cabriolet, chasis no. 003 of the first series.

A round 1950 a well-to-do client and industrialist ordered a convertible built according to his own wishes on a Packard Eight. Apparently he did not like the wide front grilles and the slab-sided forms, which became the fashion of the time. Thus a stately two-door cabriolet with the tall, traditional, erect grille with big headlamps on either side was completed. The stretched – but still clearly shaped – fenders, front and rear, distantly resembled the Lincoln

gant design was completed. With its 2.4-liter four-cylinder engine producing 100 hp, this English sports car would top 100 mph. Apart from a few dyed-in-the-wool Porsche enthusiasts, it is nearly forgotten that Beutler coachbuilt a total of six cabriolets on the very early Porsche 356. These 356s were made in Gmünd, Austria. One of the very first to be completed was shown at the Geneva Automobile Salon of 1949. The oldest extant serial-production Porsche 356 with chassis number 003 is the property of a lucky Swiss enthusiast.

Soon thereafter a cabriolet on the astonishingly fast and well-handling Lancia Aprilia chassis was delivered. The advanced technical concept and the excellent road qualities of this model made it a darling with coachbuilders and connoisseurs alike.

Probably the first coupé made by Beutler was on the British Bristol 401 chassis, which had a 2-liter six-cylinder engine originally of BMW design. The long, swept line of the front fender, reaching to the rear end of the car, was praised as especially elegant by the Swiss weekly *Automobil Revue*. Above the waistline the car was lacquered in a light color, an effort to make it look lighter. An Austin A90 chassis obtained a 2/4-seat cabriolet body. It did not yet show a pure slab-sided form and had a fairly long tail. These Beutler bodies generally resembled the creations of the French coachbuilders in the last years prior to the war.

Two Bristol 401 models, a coupé from 1949 (top left) and a cabriolet from 1950 (top right and this story's leading photo). Above: Beutler wasn't confined to Europe. The coachbuilder also bodied this 1950 Packard Eight cabriolet.

Continental of the immediate postwar years. The classic and rather severe lines gave the somewhat heavy-looking car a noble look. The cabriolet was lacquered in light grey, had a black leather upholstery and a black top. For a number of years it could be found parked on the streets of Berne, the Swiss capital city.

Next, a cabriolet on the Jowett Jupiter chassis was finished. It heralded the advent of the modern lines. With its flat sides, where the rear fenders were only scantly marked, and the low-set and wide grille, it is obvious that Ernst Beutler had taken a long look at the creations of the top Italian coachbuilders. In these years new design ideas had increasingly imposed themselves with the famous companies across the Alps. Little wonder, therefore, that the Beutler-Jowett was immediately successful in a Swiss concours d'elégance.

The fine chassis of the Bentley was considered by several Swiss coachbuilders as the *non-plus-ultra*. The Mark VI Beutler 4/5-seat cabriolet with up-to-date, slab-sided body was very expensive, costing more than $10,000 in 1951. On this car it is clearly visible that the modern design was not yet fully mastered. Despite its two-color lacquering the car seems too heavy. This unique car also is still in the collection of a Swiss connoisseur.

Another project on a notable English chassis occurred in 1952, when Beutler built a cabriolet on the revolutionary Jaguar XK 120 chassis, a body style not yet available from the factory. As with most other coachbuilders, Beutler found it difficult to top the unique body lines of the standard roadster and coupé. It, too, was a bit on the heavy side. One year later at the Geneva Salon the company produced and displayed a new cabriolet on the big Jaguar Mk VII chassis. It unmistakably shows the design pen of Ernst Beutler. (This car survives in France.) Also at the Salon, but on the Lancia stand, there was a Beutler-made cabriolet on the new Aurelia platform. It was lacquered in an exotic two-color scheme and remained a solitaire.

At the Geneva Salon of 1954 Beutler surprised the automobile press and experts with a 2/4-seat VW coupé. Its appearance and smooth body lines did not give any hint, at first sight, that the car was rear-engined. In the following years this model was built in small series. VW launched only a coupé in 1956, not built by Beutler but rather, as is well known, by Karmann-Ghia. From France, the body of the standard Citroën FWD "traction" by now unquestionably showed definite signs of aging. Yet Beutler developed a handsome coupé on the most powerful version, which had a six-cylinder engine. The model was a bit too pricey for its field and did not lead to serial production.

Ernst Beutler chose the Aurelia B55 platform to create an attractive cabriolet the next year. The B55's brilliant technical design included the first production V6 engine, the De Dion rear-axle with the gearbox in unity with the differential, and fabulous road-holding. The Lancia Aurelia's package contributed to its success in sports car racing. The work offered the America Spider, but no cabriolet.

Left: 1951 Bentley Mk VI cabriolet. Right: Jowett Jupiter cabriolet.

as well to buy and drive one of the famous sports cars from Stuttgart. While the cooperation with the work was friendly, nobody at Porsche was seriously thinking of taking up the Beutler coupé as a standard body version.

Bristol was no longer regularly imported into Switzerland. Still, the company asked Beutler to produce a prototype with a 2/4-seat coupé on the model 406E. This was the last version with the trusted six-cylinder engine, which was now bored out to 2.2 liters. Probably to test the market, the Bristol-Beutler coupé was listed in Switzerland at 39,750 Swiss Francs (approx. $9,350). While no close cooperation resulted from this prototype it is interesting to note how the later Bristol models with big V8 engines show many features of the proposed Beutler body.

In 1959 visitors of the Geneva Salon were surprised to find a Citroën ID 19 converted into a cabriolet by Beutler. The metal roof was simply cut off and replaced by a fully disappearing rag top. Rumors have it that the rear doors on the exhibition car were welded solid – in order to increase stability. Whether there was just one prototype or more is not quite clear. It is a fact, however, that Ernst Beutler had seen the writing on the

Top: Beutler bodied BMW 502/503 coupés from 1957-59. Above (left to right): 1958 VW-Porsche 356 coupé; 1959 Citroën ID 19 cabriolet; 1959 Auto Union 1000 coupé.

OTHER SUCCESSFUL PRODUCTIONS

In the annual *Automobil Revue* of 1957, Gebrüder Beutler & Co. placed an advertisement showing a new and very smart-looking coupé on the powerful and expensive BMW 502 chassis. The V8 engine with 3.2-liter capacity delivered 120 hp. It is said that

a total of six similar cars were built, partly on the 503 chassis with the power increased to 140 hp. Beutler changed the front design, which originally had a wide, low-set grille, to the more traditional, classic BMW double-kidney shape.

In 1958 the little Simca Aronde coupé by Beutler was completed. The popular Porsche 356B coupé was also launched, which in the following years was also produced in small series. It allowed the family father

wall very early. Unfortunately it did not bring the company much profit. Two years later Citroën launched their cabriolet on the market – built by Chapron.

Above: 1958 Bristol 406 prototype coupé. Below: This Bugatti T.57 sports a replica body built in 1970.

THE END OF COACHBUILT SPECIAL MODELS

The demand for special bodies had dwindled in Switzerland in the 1960s. One company after another had to give up this branch in their works. Only Hermann Graber (see *Automobile Quarterly*, Vol. 41 No. 3) continued briefly with Alvis and Rover chassis to serve a very small market.

Out of necessity Gebrüder Beutler & Co. changed its activities to the repair of car bodies. Around 1970 they unexpectedly obtained an order to produce a replica body for a classic Bugatti Type 57 of prewar days. The cabriolet was built according to an original Jean Bugatti drawing that was never used in the factory in Molsheim. It was used with slight modification by Carrosserie Worblaufen, and the final work gives full credit to the ability of the small company. It is a very handsome creation and the quality of workmanship is superb, a car not only pleasing to the owner and now his son, but also a highlight in many meetings of classic cars in Switzerland.

Fritz Beutler died in 1986 and one year later the company closed. Ernst retired but continued to take much interest in cars, driving his beloved Beutler-Porsche coupé. In 2000, as he celebrated his 85th birthday, a meeting was organized by the Swiss Car Register in which the owners of most of the surviving Beutler-coachbuilt cars participated. Ernst Beutler died in 2005, but many of his creations will remind us of the wonderful work he and his staff performed over the course of 40 years. AQ

1955 Lancia Aurelia B55 cabriolet.

Detail Man
Art Gallery with Dan McCrary

I f the devil's in the details, Dan McCrary will tell you that revelation is as well, whether in a reflection off shiny, smooth chrome or in a shadow underlying faded, peeling paint. In his quest to set his art apart with unique compositional techniques, this artist achieves eye-stopping results that show familiar subjects in unique and interesting ways.

Left: "Speedster and friend".

BY TRACY POWELL

Dan McCrary was hooked on cars at an early age. His earliest memories consist of the noise of revving engines, the smell of gasoline, the cheers of crowds, and the sights of cars blurring past during stock car races at the old speedway in Raleigh, N.C. He went with his family when he was 5 and 6. All the noise and color and action of the races, combined with what was going by on the streets every day – the colors and the chrome of the '50s era – caught his eye.

McCrary was born in Raleigh in 1949. Although the old speedway in Raleigh didn't last long past the late

and drew, everything that I drew revolved around a car. I don't remember drawing anything else. Other kids would draw airplanes in the sky, maybe a war scenario with dotted lines going from the planes shooting something. With me it was always a car."

Speed Age was another popular magazine in those days, and McCrary began noticing other types of racing cars than stock cars. That publication covered midgets, sprints and Indy cars. Unbeknownst to him, McCrary was gradually picking up all these different types of influences, "without dropping the previous ones. It became more and more of this addictive stuff."

home for ingestion, the impressionable youth was influenced again, this time with the combination of sports cars and road racing.

"I was always in the 'all of the above' enthusiast group," McCrary said. "I liked hot rods, sports cars and race cars of all kinds. Some time in high school

Left: "Boyle special." Above: "Back to Nature."

1950s, McCrary's interest in cars did.

"Once I picked up the 'habit' it stuck with me," McCrary said. "My first experience with cars in magazines goes back to the days when you could buy *Custom Cars* or *Rod & Custom* for a quarter, when they were in small format. At that point I discovered hot rods and custom cars. All this time, as kids doodled

McCrary also had an aunt who lived in an older section of Raleigh, in a Victorian house with neighbors who parked their "funny little car" in the driveway. The little car immediately captured young McCrary's attention; it turned out to be a Triumph TR3. Visiting his aunt's house also meant access to stacks of *Road & Track*, found on tables and the floor. Taking copies

I copied what I saw in magazines and tried to execute them in color. I was using colored ink or markers."

Living in the South, hot rods or customs could be spied being fixed up in back yards, but to actually see one was rare. Unlike the experience of growing up in Southern California where they were everywhere, "It was an exotic thing to actually see one on the street. So it was like seeing another world through the pages of a magazine that featured hot rods."

Into the Music Scene

When McCrary was a sophomore or junior in high school, he and several of his friends, who were also car nuts, raced slot cars together in a vacant room at a friend's house. In that room was a guitar, leaning in a corner. The boys would take turns amateurishly playing it, "and that led to a detour. All us car guys got guitars for Christmas and we started a band."

The guitar literally struck a chord with McCrary – it became his chosen instrument. He and his pals played together for the rest of high school, and the pastime extended into college days after McCrary entered East Carolina University without a declared major. The weekends spent playing in bands got longer and longer;

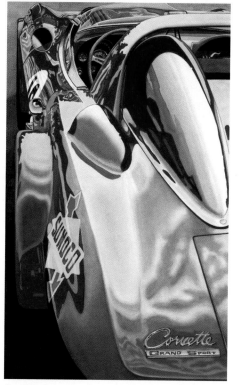

Top: "Ted Horn's Baby." Left: "Sculpt Merc." Above: "Ain't it Grand."

87

instead of leaving on Friday and coming back Monday, he was leaving Thursday and coming back Tuesday. It got to the point after about a year and half of college McCrary had dropped out and was playing music full time, jamming with The Prophets based in Greenville.

Then, "I was aware that there was a war going on in Southeast Asia," McCrary said. He was drafted and spent two years in the Army stationed in Germany. After his service, he returned to college fully intending to major in art. But the old pattern took hold once again, and the college student played music with increasing frequency and success. After a couple of quarters of study, he was back in a band full time and college was put on hold. One thing was different this time around, however; this time he met his wife. All

along, McCrary never lost his automotive passion.

"Before the war I had a '55 Chevy with a 327 in it. Over in Europe I saw all these cool-looking Alfas running around and I got hooked on those. I bought the first Alfa I saw when I got home."

An invitation to again play in a band after his Army stint led the McCrarys to Charlotte, where they still live and work. After a few years of playing in this newly formed group, the near-constant regimen of setting up, playing and tearing down, gig after gig, finally led McCrary to settle down at a "normal" job. That job was in a music store in Charlotte. At that time, in 1977-78, McCrary owned a 1969 Alfa Romeo Duetto that was being worked on at a body shop, the lobby in which McCrary had placed a few car drawings.

For those pen-and-ink drawings McCrary had used colored ink. It was at this body shop that McCrary met a Porsche owner who had noticed the drawings – and who commissioned McCrary's first paid artwork.

"He gave me money to do his 911. That first commission planted a seed that somebody would actually pay me for this. Much to the music store manager's chagrin, I had sports car enthusiasts walking into the store to pick up their freshly executed car portraits."

With no more weekends committed to traveling between music gigs, McCrary soon took up the same Porsche owner's suggestion to race his Alfa in regional autocross events. That led to mixing with Sports Car Club of America (SCCA) members, opening the door to a new market for McCrary's art.

Above: "The Doors." Right: "Forty Fun House."

"Fun Haus Mirror."

"Raindrops Keep Falling."

Above: "Exhausted Duesenberg." Below: "Unliner."

"What makes painting cars fun is when the make and model of a car becomes almost irrelevant," McCrary said, "except for the fact that particular shapes and details converge to become a specific year and model. That notion becomes secondary to the abstract notion of this cluster of angles and shapes and colors and so forth, which really captures the eye. We may never totally achieve it, but it's worth striving to create something that people will buy as a piece of art versus just a painting of a car that they once owned. I'm not invalidating that reason for purchasing a painting, but you want them to take a deeper look and see it the same way the artist saw it.

"It's a sign that I've been successful as an artist if somebody's basing their purchase – or even making a compliment – on the painting itself, rather than because they have the car's shop manual and color chips and everything else they collect that goes with the car."

PASSION PLAY

McCrary still plays guitar, although just "very occasionally." He'd like to be able to play more often – with a part-time rhythm and blues band, ideally – but his packed schedule doesn't allow for much other than painting. The preferred pace can be described as "packed and loaded" – McCrary was working on 12 different paintings at once when this interview took place: one was a Cord sedan for the Gilmore Car Museum; one was a pile of '57 Chevy fenders and bumpers arranged in an abstract jumble; a close-up of a Ferrari F40's hood and front fender graced another canvas; another was a close-up of a dash; and yet another canvas featured a vintage NASCAR scene, a '53 Olds pitting at Langhorne.

"My interests are still so varied and broad, I skip from painting to another when one gets a little tedious," McCrary said. "It's part of what keeps the juices going for me. Tom Hale once told me that I was like a kid in a candy store in terms of not nailing down any one area of interest – I'm just scattered all over the place."

His medium of choice is watercolor due to its transparency, among other aesthetic attributes. Before using watercolors, McCrary was adept with pen-and-ink until another artist informed him that his colored inks would eventually fade. That led to experimentation and the transition to watercolor, a medium that McCrary "fell into" in his search for new methods and materials. McCrary is a member of the National Watercolor Society.

"With watercolor, I love the way you can capture the essence of what's going on in the sheetmetal and so forth." That goes for commissions and private work alike. "As cars become more and more generic, it's nice to preserve the history, the look and the style – the emotional feeling you get – when you look at some of these older vehicles where style didn't necessarily follow function."

"I Believe I Can Fly."

"Snake in the Grass."

Much of this sentiment is not wasted on McCrary, who notes that his work has much to do with a larger effort to preserve this attitude, to "keep alive something that's going by the boards." McCrary sees two extremes, both intricately woven in the passion for historical automotive preservation. Walking around a junkyard for hours on end, shooting rolls of film for reference, extols as much enjoyment as the same task at Meadow Brook or Amelia Island concours events.

"I don't exalt one over the other in terms of my fascination," McCrary said. "After all these years I still haven't hit that point where I've become blasé or jaded about any of it. It's still all kind of fresh: going to a concours, setting up a few paintings, and rushing out with my camera to see what kind of goodies are out there. There's always that sense of anticipation."

"The thing that gets me going is the close-up image, whether the car is rusty or shiny. I like the abstract quality it takes on when you get in close on a corner that has a sculpted area on, say, a '50s car with a fin and the chrome. It all combines and you can make an abstract sense of composition using a realistic technique."

Working in Charlotte, the heart of NASCAR country, one would think that McCrary's portfolio would be crowded with Sunday afternoon personalities and their ad-laden cars. Not so for McCrary. But one of his favorite commissions of late was of racer Rusty Wallace. The painting was commissioned by Penske general manager Don Miller for Wallace's retirement, a montage consisting of about a dozen of the driver's career milestones.

"It went from his first stock car, with primer-and-duct-tape numbers, all the way up to what he was driving when he retired," McCrary said. "It was really neat to do something like that for somebody like that, and have it presented at their Christmas party. Things like that come along once in a while and are unique enough to be a novelty for me."

GLOBAL VISION

ART CENTER COLLEGE OF DESIGN

*T*oday's complex automotive marketplace demands designers with a wide spectrum of skills. Buick now sells more cars in China than in America. Buick's 2007 Riviera concept was created at GM's design center in China and unveiled at the Shanghai Auto Show. Toyota, who sold their first car in the United States in 1957, designs cars in Southern California and has passed GM to become the world's largest automaker. The automotive world has been turned upside down. Designers entering the industry today must be prepared with a global vision, and Art Center College of Design fulfills its mandate to produce such designers, as it has for nearly 75 years.

BY LEIGH DORRINGTON

Automobile design evolved quite naturally from the carriage-building trade. Just as early "horseless carriages" were nothing more than carriages with rudimentary gasoline, electric or steam engines attached to wooden frames, the need first to enclose and, then, to distinguish one automobile from another relied heavily on the existing trade. Various body styles built on automobiles – cabriolets, phaetons, sedans – were carriage styles first.

Carriage building was a craft. The elegant designs, wood framing, fine fabrics, leather, glass and metals and the lustrous finishes were the work of skilled artisans who learned their craft through apprenticeships and years of practice. Concours d'elegance were an opportunity for carriage builders and their wealthy patrons to show off their newest styles on the avenues of Paris each spring.

Carriage makers soon filled a niche in the burgeoning automobile industry as well. Early automobiles were affordable by only the wealthiest. And, as with their carriages, owners of fine automobiles sought to distinguish their automobiles and themselves. Harley J. Earl, who is often credited with inventing automobile styling, began working in his father's successful coach and carriage company in Los Angeles (*Automobile Quarterly*, Vol. 20 No. 1), which became the Earl Automobile Works in 1908. The Earl company soon found an enthusiastic and free-spending clientele with the new Hollywood community, as did Walter M. Murphy Motors in Pasadena.

As automobiles entered mass production and became more accessible to everyone the owners' desire to differentiate themselves didn't diminish, it increased. The auto industry turned to people like Earl and others who had been successful with the silk stocking trade.

Earl was hired by General Motors to head the Art & Colour Section in 1927. The same year Edsel Ford, the only son of Henry Ford and who was credited with impeccable taste, was actively involved with the design of body styles for the new Ford Model A. The Model A – with its variety of body styles and colors – saved the Ford Motor Company, which had grown moribund after 20 years of Model T production and limited color choices.

The new field of industrial design with its proponents like Raymond Loewy successfully applied their talents to automotive design. Ford created a styling section under E.T. "Bob" Gregorie and Chrysler created their own in-house styling group, albeit in a corner of the vaunted engineering department. Smaller automakers hired talented individuals, like Gordon Buehrig, or contracted for the services of industrial design firms. Loewy began working with Studebaker in 1938 and established a full styling studio inside of Studebaker's headquarters in South Bend, Ind.

Training of designers, or stylists, took place in a variety of ways but the most common was on the job. Some noted designers took their skills from one manufacturer to another, like Buehrig who worked at Packard, Stutz, Auburn, Cord and Duesenberg, and

Left: Instructor Joseph Thompson viewing a student's clay model of a car as the student works on the model, circa 1949.
Right: Students at work on a clay model of a car with George Jergenson observing, 1949.

retired from Ford in 1965. Others, like Bill Mitchell at General Motors, were trained and spent their entire careers with one manufacturer.

As the industry grew, a need for schools to train automotive designers before they would be hired by automakers became apparent. Industrial design schools like Pratt Institute in New York created transportation design courses. Others, like the University of Cincinnati, combined a transportation track with cooperative working experience. Another one of the early innovators was the Art Center School in Los Angeles.

ART CENTER

Art Center College of Design in Pasadena has perhaps trained more of the designers in the automobile industry than any other school.

In an era in which retired GM vice president of design Wayne Cherry describes top designers as "rock stars," a list of Art Center graduates reads like the equivalent of the Rock and Roll Hall of Fame. Chris Bangle of BMW is an Art Center graduate. Hot-rodder extraordinaire Chip Foose studied at Art Center. So did J Mays, chief creative officer of Ford, and Freeman Thomas, head of Ford's advanced design studio in Irvine, Calif. Mark Jordan, designer of the iconic Mazda Miata and son of another retired GM vice president of design, Chuck Jordan, is a graduate. Superstars all.

Not to mention Cherry, who managed throughout the most prolific period of design innovation in GM history (*Automobile Quarterly*, Vol. 46 No. 3); Richard Teague, who was highly regarded as vice president of design for American Motors in the late 20th century; or Strother MacMinn, who studied and taught at Art Center, worked in the industry and pioneered the school's close ties with the automobile industry.

But Transportation Design is only one area in which Art Center prepares outstanding working professionals. A Who's Who of creative stars studying here include: Chuck Queener, automotive illustrator, book designer and Ferrari aficionado; Frank Nuovo, chief of design at Nokia; and Roger Avary, movie director, producer and Oscar-winning script writer for "Pulp Fiction."

The Art Center School was founded in Los Angeles in 1930 with 12 faculty and eight students. Founder Edward A. "Tink" Adams was an advertising executive who envisioned a school to train artists and designers for the real-world needs of the advertising, publishing and industrial design fields. Adams' philosophy, described as revolutionary at the time but widespread today, was to build a "faculty of professionals rather than a professional faculty." This method immediately proved its worth in the difficult years that soon followed and the school claimed a 97-percent job-placement rate in the Depression era.

Veterans returning from WWII also found the school's emphasis on job preparation to their liking as they were in a hurry to join the postwar boom. The school soon

Left: John Coleman advising a student who is at work on a transportation drawing of a car, circa 1951.
Above: George Jergenson instructing a class of transportation students, circa 1951.

offered year-round instruction, and increasing enrollment caused a move to a larger Los Angeles campus in 1946. In 1949 the Art Center School was accredited to offer bachelor's degrees in Industrial Design, Photography, Illustration and Advertising.

A seminal event in 1955 strongly influenced the future of the school. Adams and the chairs of the transportation and product design programs were invited by the Japanese government to tour postwar Japan and lecture on industrial design. According to David F. Lynn, one of the few scholars who have studied the genesis of automotive design education, "This trip forged a bond between the Japanese manufacturers and Art Center that began a steady flow of the country's brightest designers back and forth to the school and was a significant step toward making Southern California the automotive center that it is today."

The name of the school was changed to Art Center College of Design in 1965. Continuous growth in all fields of study created the need to move once again to the current Pasadena Hillside Campus in 1976 and the subsequent expansion to the South Campus in 2004.

The South Campus also hosts Art Center's Public Programs. Programs including Art Center at Night, Saturday High and Art Center for Kids contribute to the vitality of the community and provide an opportunity to study with Art Center faculty. Other programs, like the Design-Based Learning Lab for K-12 educators and the Entrepreneurial Studies program, are designed for professional development.

The tradition of a faculty of professionals has also continued as a cornerstone of the Art Center education. Photographer Ansel Adams taught briefly at Art Center in the early days. Ken Okuyama – formerly creative director at Pininfarina S.p.A. where he designed the Ferrari Enzo – was also chair of the Art Center Transportation Department.

Today Art Center offers undergraduate degrees in majors including Advertising, Environmental Design, Film, Fine Arts Media, Graphic Design, Illustration, Photography and Imaging, Product Design and Transportation Design. Graduate programs are also offered in Film, Art, Industrial Design, Media Design, Criticism and Theory. The school currently has an

Above: Strother MacMinn and his class, 1960. Center: MacMinn advising students who are at work on preparing small-scale wind tunnel models of cars for a test at Caltech (left to right): Wayne Cherry, who graduated in 1961; MacMinn; and Leon Goldik, who graduated in 1962. Far right: Clay is still used in modeling at Art Center, as it is throughout the industry, from surface molding to milling.

Art Center has evolved with the times, in instruction, technology and facilities. Above is Art Center's campus at 2544 7th St., Los Angeles in 1945; below is the campus at night as it looks today.

enrollment of approximately 1,650, including 1,500 undergraduates and 150 graduate students. Fewer than 10 percent of Art Center students are enrolled in the Transportation Design major.

THE HOUSE THAT MAC BUILT

No other person in the history of Art Center has been more closely associated or contributed more to the Transportation Design program than Strother MacMinn. "Mac" was one of the most influential people in international automobile design (*Automobile Quarterly*, Vol. 37, No. 4). He was also a part of Art Center for 63 years before passing away in 1998. He was an Art Center student, as well as a teacher, historian, writer, photographer, concours judge, raconteur and valued friend.

He created the Art Center Transportation Design program in 1948. He was one of the Art Center Representatives who traveled to Japan in 1955 and

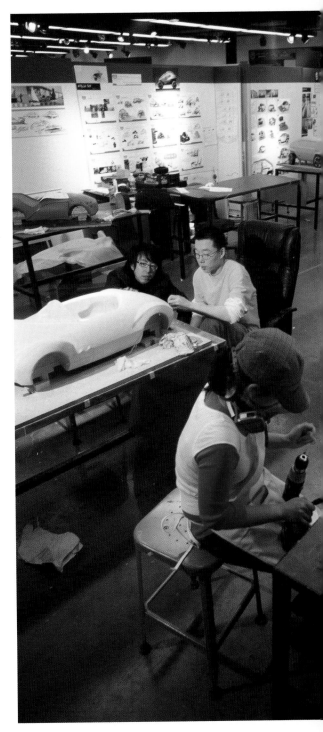

worked throughout five decades to establish close ties between Art Center and automakers.

In 1985, 50 years after he entered Art Center as a student, MacMinn wrote a history of "Walter M. Murphy, Coach Builders" in Pasadena (*Automobile Quarterly*, Vol. 23 No. 4). The story described the origin of the styling industry, the unique influence of the Southern California environment on automobile design and the weight of international perspective, as it was fully half a century before the industry began to recognize itself as competing in a global marketplace. His own design education began in Pasadena when he was 12 years old and rode his bicycle to Walter M. Murphy Motors, where he introduced himself to chief designer Frank Hershey.

Just six years later MacMinn was working for Hershey at General Motors' Art & Colour Section in Detroit. He later joined the notable industrial design office of Henry Dreyfuss and for more than 45 years taught at Art Center and worked as an independent designer. He worked as a consultant to Toyota Motor Corporation beginning in 1963 and helped to establish Toyota's Calty Design Research center in Newport Beach in 1972, a resource that has been duplicated by virtually every other automaker the past 30 years.

Before his death he spoke about the joy he found in teaching at Art Center: "There is no stronger reinforcement for real values than to share the enthusiasm of young designers who are sincerely career-oriented. It's a never-ending privilege and delight."

THE ART CENTER EXPERIENCE

If Art Center students are distinguished for their accomplishments, so too is their learning experience for its rigor. Prospective students are required to select a major field of study as part of the application process and to submit a portfolio prior to an admission decision. It is unusual for Art Center students to change majors once they have been enrolled. David Lynn notes, "Shopping for a major is a very rare occurrence at Art Center. A more likely scenario is shopping for a different institution."

Coursework is planned for eight terms but most students take more time, including terms when they are participating in internship programs or not enrolled. The accelerated year-round curriculum is designed to make it possible to graduate in less than three years, however. The first four terms include fundamentals and core requirements, while the second four terms are designed to put students' learning into intense studio practice. Arts & Science requirements have been added to the curriculum, but in addition to – not in place of – any part of the rigorous design requirements. Students balance core requirements such as English composition, math, history, natural and social sciences with design studies. Per Volquartz, an Art Center graduate and former teacher says, "Art Center is grueling – it is like medical school without the blood."

Art Center creates an environment of collaboration and competition, just as students will find following graduation. Portfolio reviews take place again at the end of the third term and the sixth term, and these are sometimes a watershed experience causing students to re-evaluate the suitability of Art Center for their continuing education.

Not least among the significant challenges to Art Center students is the cost, which is currently $14,000 per term for tuition only. The cost of tuition for an undergraduate degree in eight terms is over $110,000 plus the significant costs for materials, housing, food and transportation in the Los Angeles area, although sources of financial aid are available.

As a result, Art Center attracts students who are motivated, eager to work and to learn. The average entering age of Art Center undergraduates is 23. Ninety percent have previously attended another college, and some fulfill academic requirements before enrolling at Art Center. Nearly 20 percent have earned a prior college degree. Previous Art Center students acknowledge the experience leaves little time for extracurricular activities but use words like "dream" and "worth it" to describe their education.

Art Center College of Design is perennially ranked as the top design school in the United States for both undergraduate and graduate programs.

"Back in the time when I went to Art Center it was the school that auto designers came from," said Wayne Cherry. "In Harley Earl's time, they trained their own. GM was an academy: it trained a lot of (designers) who went on to other companies." But as the influence of design grew within the auto industry and competitive pressures forced Ford, Chrysler and other automakers to create their own styling departments, the need for designers grew.

Art Center graduates were trained to do the work. In addition to ideation and drafting, Art Center students learned and practiced critical skills in rendering, clay modeling and presentation. Graduates stood out for their skill in producing finely finished illustrations. "I was the only one from my class hired by GM (in March 1962)," Cherry recalled. "Other designers from different backgrounds had started six months ahead of me, but I was asked to help evaluate their work.

"The difference today is that there are a lot of schools in transportation design, and there are a lot more companies hiring designers. There were basically three companies hiring designers in the U.S. when I started. Now there are companies worldwide [looking

Tomorrow's automotive design directions are already taking shape in the minds and imaginations of Art Center's current crop of students.

at the same talent] and there are more schools, too. There are schools in Paris, Moscow – there's one in Korea – I don't even know them all."

But he is well qualified to speak on the subject. Cherry was the first vice president of design at GM who spent most of his career working outside of the United States before he became the head of GM Design. As vice president of design beginning in 1992 he continued work started at GM by Chuck Jordan to create digital studios, developed holographic virtual design presentations that could be viewed simultaneously in GM studios worldwide. And he hired designers from outside of GM. Simon Cox, Anne Asensio and others not only brought experience from working at different companies but from different educational backgrounds and cultures as well.

GM and other automakers also hire designers from other U.S. schools. Pratt Institute, the University of Cincinnati, the College for Creative Studies (CCS) in Detroit, Academy of Art University in San Francisco and the Cleveland Institute of Art are all acknowledged as top schools for teaching automotive designers.

Art Center remains on the leading edge of teaching the skills required by the industry. Conceptualization, illustration, clay and foam modeling are enhanced in facilities including a 3-D modeling lab, composite and laser labs, a model shop and metal fabricating room, plus a color materials and trends exploration laboratory. Digital design tools such as UGS, Alias and Portfolio Wall software have become widely used in the industry, and a wide range of digital media tools is taught at Art Center.

Stewart Reed chairs the Transportation Design Department. Reed is an Art Center graduate and taught at the school in addition to 35 years of industry experience – including a stint as head of Toyota's Calty Research Center – before returning as chair of Transportation Design in 2005.

Reed is a cordial conversationalist who reveals an intense passion for automobiles and Art Center. He was both a student and colleague of Strother MacMinn. After completing a day of student portfolio reviews, he reflected on how Art Center students of today compare with previous generations. "Strother MacMinn was a dear friend of mine and he was an important influence to me at two or three critical times in my life. Strother – even when he was old – always had a boyish enthusiasm for what was next. We have students who are like that today. There are always those who are passionate automobile designers. They just get it.

"In the '80s we had a high number of students from South America. Now, there is a high concentration of Asian students. But those differences reflect a lot of things: economic cycles, changing markets and manufacturers' needs. This generation has grown up with computers, they use tools differently." The best, he says, always "love cars from any era. But it doesn't get in their way of being a futurist."

The Transportation Design curriculum at Art Center is designed to hone that instinctive passion. Students begin focus on the core program in the third and fourth terms. They design a complete interior and exterior. A technology class teaches the main elements of occupant layout, mechanical layout and vehicle structure.

The fifth term emphasizes "mobility research," a holistic view of human transportation needs. The course includes broader issues of safety and propulsion and may utilize the city of Pasadena as a transportation laboratory. Other transdisciplinary activities may include working with architecture students at the University of Southern California. "Student interests emerge at fifth term," Reed said.

Also in the fifth and sixth terms students can participate in Funded Educational Programs, with industry sponsors who provide students with a specific design brief. Programs have been created with BMW/DesignworksUSA, Honda, Ford and sponsors from other industries including GE Healthcare, Nokia and Nestle. Students compete to participate in a project, which may involve majors from Transportation Design and other related areas. The seventh and eighth terms are "the time of specialization," Reed said. "Some have a passion for motorcycles; some marine design.

Scholarship student and Art Center alum Wayne Cherry would go on to become the design chief at General Motors. Here he poses with an example of his work in 1961.

Instructor Bum Seuk Lim with student Carey Lyn.

Art Center encourages their interests."

Reed's Transportation Design teaching staff remains true to Tink Adams' commitment to "professionals teaching." Eight full-time faculty have design experience with Porsche Design, BMW, Honda Research and Development, Ford, Volvo, Hundai and Kia. The Transportation Design weekly faculty includes another 25 working designers from the Southern California studios of Volvo, Honda, Toyota, GM, Ford, Chrysler Pacifica and others. Reed cites 20 California design studios that Art Center draws faculty from, and refers to the Transportation Design staff as "the most powerful asset in the program."

Real-world examples of the type of designs coming from Art Center is seen above as the ultra-modern, ultra-sleek Cunningham C7 sedan and below as a scale model of a crossover concept.

Art Center has always believed in intense collaboration with industry leaders, all to involve students and faculty with the latest technological and engineering developments. Above: The IndyCar 2011 project. Right: The 2007 Car Classic event.

DESIGNING FOR THE REAL WORLD

Art Center students also participate in activities that sustain the school's founding emphasis on real-world experience. One recent example is the Bugatti Project, a Funded Educational Project sponsored by collector Peter Mullin, whose gleaming, restored Type 64 chassis sits in the project studio. Ettore Bugatti's son Jean completed preliminary body designs for the chassis, which were never built. Mullin owns the original drawings in addition to the restored chassis. The design brief for the project challenged students to create a body for the Mullin chassis using Jean Bugatti's designs as inspiration. One selected design will be constructed and displayed suspended above the chassis in the new museum Mullin is creating for his collection.

The Indianapolis Motor Speedway and Indy Racing League sponsored the IndyCar 2011 project in anticipation of the 100th Indianapolis 500 in 2011. Twenty-five students from Transportation Design, Environmental Design, Product Design and Illustration/Entertainment Design worked in transdisciplinary teams. Their brief was to design a hallmark Indy car for the future, as well as extensions into fan experience and entertainment such as real-time motion simulators and video games. "Much of the history of the Indianapolis 500 and the sport have come from Southern California," said Terry Angstadt, president, commercial division for the IRL. "Both history and the future intersect there, and the ideas and creativity that come from this project can help address our future in creative and energetic ways."

The Art Center College of Design Spring Show displays work of graduating students in the undergraduate Transportation Design program. Graduating seniors prepare and present projects based on research to determine needs of actual automakers and vehicles.

The show is highly professional and includes styling models and promotional materials created to a high standard.

Eighth term student Stacie Passarelli's project is typical. Each eighth term Transportation Design student researches the auto industry to independently identify an area of opportunity as the subject of his or her project. The project also contributes to a professional portfolio to help in seeking a job after graduation.

During her Art Center studies, Passarelli created projects for Ford, Volkswagen and BMW. She recognized the need to complement her portfolio with a project for an Asian automaker and her research identified a new rear-wheel-drive platform being developed by Hundai. Her project created a two-seat roadster to fill a niche in the Hundai product mix based on the new platform. With only four weeks remaining before graduation, her project was well defined by the sketch wall displayed behind her clay model. The exhibit profiled the target consumer, interpreted Hundai design language and the proposed direction for her roadster. The exhibit also defined the design "architecture" that determined placement of the occupants and mechanical components as her clay model took final shape on the table.

Passarelli is also a typical Art Center Transportation Design student. She completed a bachelor's degree in biology at Dennison University in Ohio and worked in the medical field before studying at Art Center. "My grandmother always encouraged me to pursue my creative interests, and here I am," she explained, smiling.

Fellow eighth term student Attila Tay applied tape to define the grille area of his project nearby. His project, identified as Infiniti Q65, is a proposal for a luxury flagship sedan that he calls "Dark Star". A sketch wall also displayed the process he worked through before progressing to the clay model. The occupant layout is surrounded with finely finished illustrations of the completed vehicle, including various rear fender shapes explored before selecting the final iteration he is modeling. Tay is a native of Malasia and completed his Art Center degree after studying in the United States for seven years.

Columbian Leon Paz's project is a crossover Renault Sudamerica, designed for South American markets. His sketch wall displayed outlines of the Sudamerica on the Nissan Murano, which it would compete against, while he described the project to a visitor to the studio.

Inspiring examples of rolling art is also seen at Car Classic, Art Center's annual automotive open house in July. Visitors from the industry, collectors, participants in related design fields, and enthusiasts gather to view a concours-style display of significant automobiles in the Sculpture Garden. "Dream Machines", "Coachbuilding", "Legends" and "Supercars" have headlined recent shows.

Car Classic began in 2003 and has quickly grown with a high level of student involvement to become a world-class event. In addition to displaying featured automobiles, well-known designers – including Art Center alumni and faculty – are invited to describe how their designs progressed from concept to fin-

Above: One of the clay models under construction as part of the Bugatti Project.

ished automobile. Peter Brock, Reeves Callaway, Dan Gurney, Henrik Fisker, Gordon Murray and restorer Randy Ema have been among the presenters. Over 100 extraordinary automobiles are displayed each year before a select crowd that includes top automotive designers and collectors from around the world. Visitors are invited into the Art Center building, where they can observe studio and lab facilities, the Student Gallery, current projects and talk with students.

DESIGNING FOR THE FUTURE

Art Center president Richard Koshalek also challenges students to consider, "Will my work really make a difference on a global level?" The Art Center education increasingly emphasizes the importance of a creative perspective and the value of those who possess it. Art Center espouses the notion that "creative people increasingly will be asked to take on the responsibility of solving real-world problems and, for the first time, function as leaders."

This direction is at the leading edge of a new concept in educating business leaders, sometimes referred to as D-Schools. *Business Week* described D-School education in 2005 as "where MBAs learn the art of blue-skying." Cases are taught with teams created to include designers and MBAs working as peers. Only a few institutions such as Stanford University currently offer programs in the field, based on the well-established model of business schools. Art Center offers a joint program that teaches the role of creativity in business decisions with the leading European business school, Insead in France.

Designmatters is a major Art Center initiative that invites transdisciplinary teams to create solutions to global challenges as varied as sustainable development, depleted natural resources and healthcare. "The responsibility of design has expanded beyond products and the market imperative. You have to deal with a much larger world," Koshalek said. Designmatters engages students, faculty and staff in an ongoing

exploration of the links between design and issues of social and humanitarian importance. The goal is to educate a new generation of designers who can advocate design as a force for positive social change.

One Designmatters project team created a proposal for integrated mobile health clinics in districts of northwest Kenya, which suffer from a lack of medical care. Key components of the proposal included an innovative multi-function pack allowing camels to transport clinics into remote areas, and the use of solar power to refrigerate medicines. Other Designmatters projects have addressed subjects as varied as a master plan for rebuilding New Orleans, designing toys to become tools for peaceful conflict resolution in the hands of children, and setting goals for building a better world by 2015 working with the U.S. headquarters for the United Nations Millennium Campaign Project.

On a distinctly lighter note, the entertainment industry also presents a unique area of opportunity for Art Center graduates. Larry Wood started his career at

Ford before moving to Mattel where he is chief designer for Hot Wheels cars. He has likely been responsible for the design of more vehicles – hundreds of millions – than any of his peers. Graduates Syd Mead ("Blade Runner", "TRON" and "Alien") and Harald Belker ("Batman & Robin", "Inspector Gadget" and "Minority Report") build vehicles for Hollywood. What goes around comes around.

Art Center College of Design enters the 60th year of educating transportation designers in 2008. Taking the occasion as an opportunity to maintain the leadership established by Strother MacMinn in 1948, the program will expand to place a greater emphasis on transportation – not only automotive design. Art Center Transportation Design graduates are already working in aircraft, motorcycle, marine, urban transportation and entertainment fields.

Art Center will continue to meet new challenges. As Koshalek noted: "At Art Center, (our) answer is to embrace change through the creation of programs and initiatives that stress the importance of design in a global context." △Q

Examples of illustrations and scale models presented at the Senior Show during spring semester, 2007.

VOLUME 47 No.2

Periodical postage paid at New Albany, Indiana, and at additional mailing offices.

CONTACTING AQ

Automobile Quarterly, ISSN 0005-1438, ISBN 1-59613-54-7 (978-1-59613-054-8), is published quarterly by Automobile Heritage Publishing and Communications, LLC. Editorial and publication offices: 800 East 8th Street, New Albany, Indiana, USA 471 50. Telephone (812) 948-AUTO (2886); fax (812) 948-2816; e-mail info@autoquarterly.com; Web site www.autoquarterly.com.

SUBSCRIPTION SERVICE

For subscriptions, back issues, indexes, reader service, changes of address, and order entry, call (866) 838-2886. If calling from Indiana or outside the U.S., call (812) 948-2886. Back issue prices start at $25.95, plus shipping. For domestic subscription orders: 1 year (4 issues), $79.95; 2 years (8 issues), $149.95; 3 years (12 issues), $199.95. for Canadian orders: 1 year, $99.95; 2 years, $189.95; 3 years, $259.95. For all other international orders: 1 year, $109.95; 2 years, $209.95; 3 years, $289.95. Mastercard, Visa, or American Express are accepted. Order online at www.autoquarterly.com. To order by mail, please send check or money order to *AQ/Automobile Quarterly*, Subscriber Services, P.O. Box 334, Stafford, TX 77497. The fax number for orders is (812) 948-2816.

POSTMASTER

Please send all changes of address to: *Automobile Quarterly*, P.O. Box 1950, New Albany, IN 47151.

OPPORTUNITY

Details of fundraising programs for car clubs and automobile museums are available by calling: (812) 948-AUTO (2886).

Cover & Contents

Art by Dan McCrary.

Frontispiece

Color photography: p.1, by Dan Bulleit.

J. Herbert Newport

The author would like to thank Kathleen Dow and her staff at the Transportation History Collection in the Special Collections Library of the University of Michigan for the introduction their Newport collection. The tapes of Newport's talks and interviews provide a special perspective, one that can only come from hearing him speak. Fred Roe graciously shared some recollections of meeting Herb Newport when he was assembling his own Duesenberg book. Stan Smith added some Floyd-Derham information, sharing research from his forthcoming duPont book. Duesenberg enthusiast Randy Ema, Jon Bill of the Auburn Cord Duesenberg Museum Library, Kim Miller of the AACA Library and Research Center, the staff of the Library of Congress in Washington, D. C., together with Mark Patrick and Barbara Thompson of the National Automotive History Collection also helped make the story possible.

Black-and-white photography: pp. 6 (top), 7, 11, 12 (left) courtesy of the J. Herbert Newport Collection, Transportation History Library, Special Collections Library, University of Michigan; pp. 6 (bottom), 9, 12 (right), 14, 15 courtesy of the Auburn Cord Duesenberg Museum.

Color photography from the AQ Photo and Research Archive.

Sam Posey

The author would like to sincerely thank Sam Posey and Ellen Greisedieck and their family for warmly welcoming him into their home, for sharing their past and their dreams.

Black-and-white photography: pp. 20, 21 (right), 28 courtesy of Sam Posey; p. 21 (left) courtesy of Elena Schouvalopf; p. 25 courtesy of Autodynamics; pp. 26, 27, 29 courtesy of Ellen Greisedieck.

Color photography: p. 18 from Artemis Images; pp. 20, 23, 28, 29, 30 courtesy of Sam Posey; pp. 22, 24, 25, 26 courtesy of Ellen Greisedieck; p. 31 (left) courtesy of Judy Greisedeick; p. 31 (right) courtesy of Leigh Dorrington.

Bibliography

Hildebrand, Grant. *Wright Space, The: Pattern and Meaning in Frank Lloyd Wright's Houses*. University of Washington Press, 1991;

Hobbs, Robert. *Edward Hopper*. New York: Harry N. Abrams, Inc., 1987;

Kimes, Beverly Rae. "John Fitch." *Automobile Quarterly*, Vol. 44 No. 2, 2004;

le Targat, Francois. *Kandinski*. New York: Rizoli International Publications, 1987;

LIFE. May 23, 1969;

McCluggage, Denise. "Hamlet in a Helmet." *Automobile Quarterly*, Vol. 1 No. 1, 1962;

Posey, Sam. *Playing with Trains*. New York: Random House, 2004;

Posey, Sam. *Mudge Pond Express, The*. New York:

BECAUSE
WOOD
IS JUST
WOOD.

Ordinary cordless drills are meant to do ordinary things, like drill into wood. To drill steel you've got to be made of something stronger. Our new cordless drill was designed from the ground up to make steel beg for mercy. It's perfectly balanced, fast and unbelievably powerful. Visit snapon.com/drillsteel for product specifications.

Snap-on.com

VOLUME 47 NO.2

G.P. Putnam's Sons, 1976;
www.americanmuralproject.com.

Cadillac's Thirty

Story excerpted from the same-titled chapter found in "Cadillac: Standard of the World" by Maurice Hendry.

All photography from the AQ Photo and Research Archives.

'57 Heaven

For their time taken for interviews, the author wishes to thank Glenn Patch, Ralph Hurley and Bob Schmidt.

All photography courtesy of '57 Heaven Museum; model shots by Dan Lyons.

Contact Information

American Bandstand Theater Complex
57 Heaven
1600 West Highway 76
Branson, MO 65616
Phone: 417-332-1960
Web site: www.AmericanBandstandTheater.com

Max Mosley

The author is grateful to Max Mosley for an interview granted in his Monte Carlo office and for early photographs. He has known his subject and followed his career since the launch of March Engineering in February of 1970. Interviewees who provided insights into the Mosley career are Robin Herd and Peter Wright. The writings of Peter Windsor, Thomas O'Keefe, Matt Bishop, Stuart Codling and Alan Henry have also been of value to this first full-length profile of Max Mosley.

Black-and-white photography: pp. 64 (left), 67, 68, 69, 70, 71 from the Ludvigsen Library; pp. 64 (right), 65, 66 courtesy of Max Mosley.

Color photography: pp. 62, 72, 73 (right), 74, 75 by Philippe Nartelli/Sport Auto; pp. 63, 73 (left) copyright Sutton Motorsport Images; p. 67 from the Ludvigsen Library.

Bibliography

de Courcy, Anne. *Diana Mosley*. London: Vintage, 2004;

Lawrence, Mike. *The Story of March*. Bourne End: Aston Publications, 1989;

Lovell, Terry. *Bernie's Game*. London: Metro Publishing, 2003;

Mosley, Diana. *A Life of Contrasts*. London: Gibson Square, 2003;

Mosley, Nicholas. *Rules of the Game and Beyond the Pale*. London: Pimlico, 1998;

Simon, Ted. *Grand Prix Year*. New York: Coward, McCann & Geoghegan, 1972.

Carrosserie Gebrüder Beutler & Co., Thun

The author wishes to extend his gratitude and appreciation to Urs Paul Ramseier and the Swiss Car Register where the remaining records of Carrosserie Beutler are part of the archives. A personal interview with Ernst Beutler in May 1998 gave precious insights into the history of the company. Correspondance with various friends and talks with owners of Beutler-bodied cars improved the knowledge on the work of the coachbuilder.

All photography courtesy of the author.

Bibliography

50 years of Swiss Coachbuilders Association 1919-1969;

75 years of Swiss Coachbuilders Association 1919-1994;

Günther, De la Rive Box & Stoop. *Schweizer Automobile*. Autovision, 1992;

Reports and articles in various motoring and automobile magazines and annuals published in Switzerland and Germany.

Art Gallery with Dan McCrary

Special thanks to this issue's artist and his very unique approach, finding beauty in the aged objects of our desire.

Contact Information

Dan McCrary
P.O. Box 18795
Charlotte, NC 28218
Phone: 704-372-2899
Fax: 704-375-8686
E-mail: mccrarydan@aol.com
www.dmccraryart.com

Serenissima

Special thanks to John G. Kaenzig of Millennium Racing GmbH for providing historical information for this interesting car.

Black-and-white photography copyright the Klemantaski Collection and Actual Photo, Bologna.

Color photography by Michel Zumbrunn.

Art Center

Sincere thanks to Chuck Queener and Reeves Callaway for helping the author find his bearings, and to Wayne Cherry, once again, for sharing his unique perspective and experiences at Art Center and General Motors. Christine Hanson and Stewart Reed of the Art Center College of Design both provided generous access to their time, Art Center materials, students and student projects. Detailed information on Art Center courses and programs is available at www.artcenter.edu. The author would also like to acknowledge the contributions to this story by David F. Lynn in his thesis "Automotive Design Education: Integrating Computer Based Tools with Traditional Techniques," Georgia Institute of Technology, August 2006. And finally, although the author never had the privilege of meeting Strother MacMinn, he is yet another student who learned the industry through Mr. MacMinn's words and images in *Automobile Quarterly* and other publications. Thank you.

All black-and-white photography courtesy of Art Center College of Design.

Color photography: pp. 104, 108-115, 118, 199 courtesy of Art Center College of Design; pp. 116, 117 by Leigh Dorrington.

Bibliography

Cherry, Wayne. Personal interview, 2007;

Lynn, David F. "Automotive Design Education: Integrating Computer Based Tools with Traditional Techniques." Georgia Institute of Technology, 2006;

MacMinn, Strother. "Fifties' Finest: Hits of the Design Decade." *Automobile Quarterly*, Volume 25 No. 1, 1987;

MacMinn, Strother. "Walter M. Murphy, Coach Builders: Daring Elegance in the Classic Era." *Automobile Quarterly*, Volume 23 No. 4, 1985;

Reed, Stewart. Personal interview, 2007;

"Strother MacMinn: 1918-1998." *Automobile Quarterly*, Volume 37 No. 4, 1998;

Witzenberg, Gary. "Design on the Road." *Automotive Traveler*, May 2007;

www.artcenter.edu.

Coda

Information provided by Bruce Wennerstrom, *AQ* subscriber and MASCDCS co-director.

Photography by Marilynn K. Yee/*The New York Times*.

Back Cover

Debossment of the Serenissima emblem from the AQ Photo and Research Archive. According to information shared by Pete Vack, the winged lion is a Christian symbol associated with St. Mark, who is buried in the Cathedral in Venice. The symbol of the city of Venice is another image of a winged lion's head with a "V" in the background. Venice was referred to as the Serene Republic before the unification, thus the name Serenissima. Count Volpi, founder of Scuderia Serenissima, was head of a prominent Venetian family.

AQ BOOK REVIEW

BENTLEY MkVI
Rolls-Royce Silver Wraith, Silver Dawn & Silver Cloud, Bentley R-Series & S-Series

By Martyn Nutland

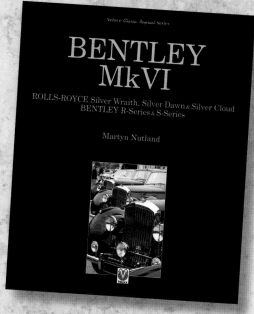

Ask any Rolls-Royce or Bentley enthusiast and they will extol these marques' last breed of "traditional" models. "Bentley MkVI" by Martyn Nutland covers these models in-depth, or at least satisfactory enough for most interested parties. It is the history of the development and production of the elegant and luxurious mainstream Rolls-Royce and Bentley models built between 1947 and 1965 that Nutland mines and presents in an easy-to-read, conversational style. The chapters are short for quick fact-checking, and each is packed with appropriate historical photography.

The story majors on the central model, the Bentley MkVI. Arguably, these models – all built on chassis, and so echoing prewar practices – were the last of the "traditional" Rolls-Royces and Bentleys. Many of these cars have survived to the present day; all are eminently collectible and very useable, even in today's traffic conditions.

This reprint of Nutland's seminal work on the Bentley MkVI and associated Rolls-Royce and Bentley models is an edition reformatted with minor revisions. (The first edition was published in 1997.) A 17-page color gallery provides a pleasant gathering of stately models. For the technically curious, appendices that identify such details as year-by-year modifications and build numbers for the various models prove most helpful.

The author is a journalist who has been covering historic motoring subjects for 43 years. He is a former editor of the Bentley Drivers Club Review.

BENTLEY MkVI
Rolls-Royce Silver Wraith, Silver Dawn
& Silver Cloud,
Bentley R-Series & S-Series
176 pages, Hardback
ISBN: 9781845840686
£ 35.00 + postage

Available from
Veloce Publishing Ltd., England
Phone: 01305 260068
Fax: 01305 268864
www.veloce.co.uk

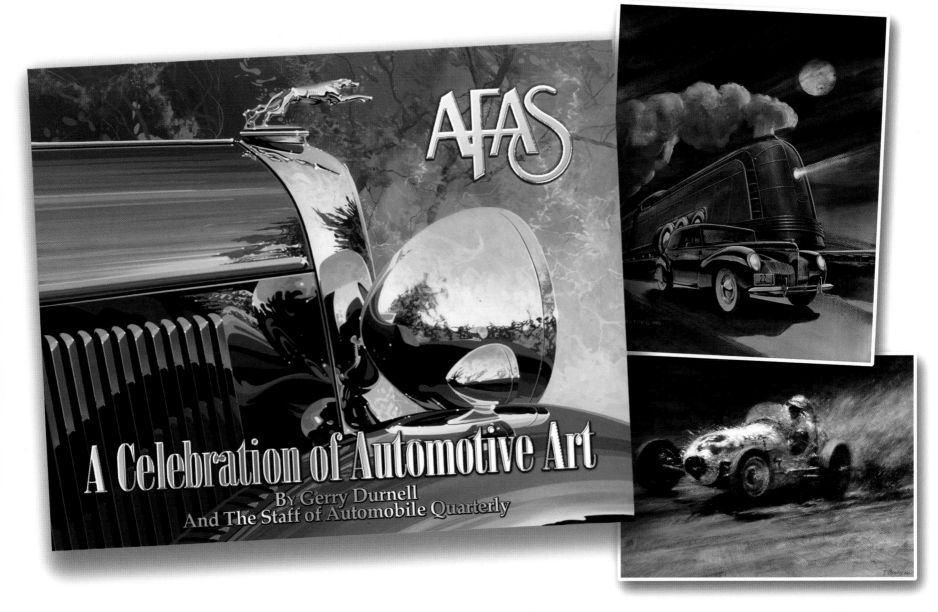

A Celebration of Automotive Art
By Gerry Durnell
And The Staff of Automobile Quarterly

A Celebration of Automotive Art

C ome meet the world's top echelon of automotive artists in Automobile Quarterly's newest book, "A Celebration of Automotive Art," a masterful compendium of the fine art and artists of the Automotive Fine Arts Society (AFAS). Articles capturing the unique personalities of all 32 artists of the AFAS are complemented by striking reproductions of their work, including the latest paintings and sculptures, available in both Deluxe Edition hardcover and autographed Collectors Edition in premium leather.

Step into the world of artistic elegance and top-shelf talent, where behind-the-canvas interviews reveal artists' impressions and philosophies. See for yourself what makes these masters tick, what stirs the passion that translates into powerful expression. This ultimate coffee-table book also covers the work and biographies of deceased Automotive Art luminaries such as Peter Helck, Walter Gotschke and Carlo Demand.

Lincoln Motor Car Co. announced the book's release at the 2005 Pebble Beach Concours d'Elegance, marking the 10-year anniversary of Lincoln sponsorship of AFAS at the event, and the Society's 20th Anniversary. More than 300 full color 11" x 14" pages presented in an attractive slipcase. Order your copy of "A Celebration of Automotive Art" today.

Specifications:

AFAS-A Celebration of Automotive Art

ISBN 1-59613-005-9 374 pages
14 x 11 (horizontal) Hardbound with slipcase

$125 + UPS shipping and handling. Call for additional Canada and International charges.

Order Today: Toll Free Phone (866) 838-2886 • Fax (812) 948-2816
Outside the U.S., call direct (812) 948-2886 • Order on our secure Web site: www.autoquarterly.com

Paul Bracq
Lawrence Braun
Melbourne Brindle
Dennis Brown
John Burgess
Harold James Cleworth
Ken Dallison
Carlo Demand
James Dietz
Ken Eberts
Art Fitzpatrick
Tom Fritz
Walter Gotschke
Tom Hale
Peter Hearsey
Peter Helck
Dennis Hoyt
Jack Juratovic
Jay Koka
Phyllis Krim
David Lord
Charles Maher
John Francis Marsh
William Motta
Niles Nakaoka
Bill Neale
Richard Pietruska
Stanley Rose
Barry Rowe
Tony Sikorski
Stanley Wanlass
Craig Warwick
Bruce Wheeler
Nicola Wood

REMEMBERING
Vince Sardi

VINCENT SARDI JR.
JULY 1915 – JANUARY 2007

For those who knew Vince Sardi, few would have been surprised to discover that his early career leanings favored medicine with plans of eventually becoming a doctor. Given his compassion and ebullient manner that later became legendary in the world of fine restaurants, the required caring personality was certainly there, though some would argue that Sardi healed more with his unmatched hospitality than most institutions of medicine. We were saddened when longtime *AQ* subscriber and the Madison Avenue Sports Car Driving and Chowder Society (MASCDCS) co-director Bruce Wennerstrom informed us of Sardi's death on Jan. 4, 2007.

As *The New York Times* reported in a lengthy obituary, "Mr. Sardi ran one of the world's most famous restaurants, a Broadway institution as central to the life of the theater as actors, agents and critics." Although his clientele of the most notoriety was the world of the theater and associated actors, producers and bit players (so much so that he was proclaimed the "Official Mayor of Broadway"), there was also a special place in his heart for the world of the automobile.

As with the legendary reputation for service and ambiance at Sardi's Restaurant, he approached his automobiles with a fierce passion. Over the years his garage entourage included a vintage drop-head Rolls-Royce named the "Draggin Wagon" that he would race at various spots such as Bridgehampton in the '50s. In 1952, a Jaguar XK120M was briefly his choice, followed by an Alfa-Romeo, which unfortunately had a reputation for breaking down, such as the time when he was leading a race at Virginia International Raceway and the driveshaft broke. Undaunted, he then moved to a 1955 modified Austin Healey 100S which he raced with great pleasure. Reflecting on the Healey association he remarked, "I really enjoyed that car. It was fun to drive and I did very well with it. I would always place either second or third, and occasionally, I would win." Later he retired, then un-retired and bought a Jaguar coupe.

Sardi was one of the founding members of the MASCDCS, which has been meeting at his restaurant for more than 50 years. His legacy of hospitality continues with his grandson Sean and partner Max Klimavicius, who extend Sardi's traditions, one of which is supporting MASCDCS meetings. It's a safe bet that he will be remembered fondly as long as the Society continues to convene.

ML   12/01